Words on Fire

on Fire

Teaching Young Writers
the Power of Words

Heidi Simmons

2017

ISBN: 978-1-938394-27-0

Library of Congress Control Number: 2017901631

Published by:
Great Life Press
Rye, New Hampshire, 03870

www.greatlifepress.com

More information is available on the Web at:
poetrylost.wordpress.com

Permissions
"The Bully" from *Baseball, Snakes and Summer Squash: Poems About Growing Up*, by Donald Graves. © 1996 by Donald Graves. Published by WordSong, an imprint of Boyds Mills Press. Used by permission.

"Poetry" from *A Writing Kind Of Day for Young Poets*, by Ralph Fletcher. © 2005 Ralph Fletcher. Published by Boyds Mills Press. Used by permission.

"Green in Spring" from *Red Sings From Treetops: A Year in Colors,* by Joyce Sidman, illustrated by Pamela Zagarenski. Text © 2009 by Joyce Sidman. Houghton Mifflin Harcourt Publishing Company. Used by permission.

For Rob . . .

and his love of words

Contents

Introduction

Words Awareness Development

"The pen is mightier than the sword" but without words the pen is useless. A child may have a story and a desire to tell it, but they cannot if they have not developed a deep appreciation and sustained curiosity for the most basic tool of writing, which is the "right" word.

Young writers progress with authors' competency as they **fire up their word choices** and give power to their story. They are challenged to fill a blank piece of paper with just the right words that satisfy their urge to communicate as well as their hope to be heard. If young writers have developed a wealth of word choice, they can be successful in finding the right word to express their thoughts.

The young writer must be motivated to build a resource of words that excite the senses; are melodious; communicate the abstract through familiar comparisons; and creatively and imaginatively interpret life's experiences. These are the words found in poetry and, therefore, it is from poetry that young writers can best build a deep well of words.

Poetry Enhances Word Awareness Development

Poetry is children's first language. They babble rhythmically. They even wail with repetitive sounds. They are immediately drawn to the fun and rhyme of Mother Goose. They enact metaphor and simile when they imagine that they are like a mother as they cradle their doll or are like a super hero when they don their capes or like a gazelle as they run across the playground. They are metaphor before they are able to pronounce the word 'metaphor.'

Since poetry is the natural language of children, it is the most relevant language for instructing young writers to learn an awed respect and deep awareness of words.

A fifth-grade student of mine best expresses the rewards of finding just the right words that reveal the thought in the following poem:

Thought

A jumbled mess
of words
fighting to get
out
rearing
writhing
whipping
lashing
striking
stabbing
beating my
head
until I write
a poem and
the thoughts
seep through
the paper
and
disappear.

Josh, 5th grade

The objective of word awareness is to inspire a young writer's sustained curiosity for words and their significance.

The instruction for word awareness is delivered through poetry, a young writer's natal language.

The reward for consistent word awareness development during the literacy block is an engaged writer and rigorous reader.

An Anecdote of Word Awareness Development

A fourth grade student serves as an example of a child extending her **word awareness development** and giving greater depth and comprehension of her own vocabulary. She uses her poetic language to scaffold her understanding of a difficult concept.

The fourth grader had just finished the book *Goin' Someplace Special, by Patricia McKissack.*

My student was particularly compassionate to the Black main character.

A summary of the book follows:

SETTING: Early 60s in the South during the Jim Crow laws.

MAIN CHARACTER: A preadolescent Black girl who begs her grandmother to go to the library alone for the first time

PROBLEM: She is naïve to the ugly prejudice outside.

RISING ACTION: She is humiliated by 1) being pushed to the back of the bus, 2) trying to sit on a park bench for whites only, 3)being shuttled out of a fancy hotel because only whites are allowed.

CLIMAX: She meets a friend of her grandmother and is reminded to "keep her head up and be strong"... so she perseveres.

.... FINALLY she arrives at the library, *Someplace Special* where chiseled in the stone over the front entrance is: "All are welcome." The main character is relieved but scared by a disillusioning cruel reality outside the library.

The challenge to my young fourth grade student was to gain an awareness of the concepts of prejudice, rejection, and innocence by connecting it to her life. The fourth grader commented on how sad and scary it must have been for the character. I offered her the word "disillusionment," and explained that it meant "huge disappointment." Using her poetic language, she took this word meaning a level deeper to a personal connection. She said, "I think her eyes are bigger than her stomach out there."

Right there through metaphor, with poignant depth and new understanding, she became personally aware of the concept of disillusionment. She had expressed that often, what we anticipate and assume will occur, fails to materialize. And when the reality is contrary to our values or beliefs, it can make us sick to our stomachs; just as trying to finish a plate piled high with too much spaghetti results in realizing we have miscalculated our hunger.

Our ten-year-old author was metaphorically expressing the misunderstood hopes and dreams encountered in growing up. Maturation is about dealing with those disappointments. She had gained an understanding of "disillusionment" through poetic interpretation. The word became hers. She would not have experienced this satisfactory new level of awareness without a practiced experience of poetic expression, which was, in this case, the use of metaphor. In the reading and writing of poetry, a child can experiment with words, and gain an understanding of them beyond their dictionary definitions.

Reading and Writing Poetry

By reading and writing poetry, word awareness is developed, language is expanded, learning is embraced and selves are empowered.

Reading

Reading poetry supports a child's natural awareness of the pleasing sounds of letters and opens opportunities for exploring the multilayered meanings of words. Early involvement in the aesthetic sound and shape of words, as well as their complexity of interpretation, encourages a child to listen and think pleasurably and critically. A word alone easily becomes a dull, simple referent. In a context, a word assumes remarkable meaning and at that moment there is critical comprehension, the ultimate objective of every reader. Poetry gives words quick accessible contexts. Many words can be explored in a short amount of time. Through noticing one's own natural and familiar play with sound and questioning word meaning, a child can establish a **serious practice** of engaging with text.

Writing

Writing poetry gives children an opportunity to directly apply this **serious practice**. Critical comprehension of language and early word play can inspire a child to create and imagine unique interpretations of the world. Every word in a poem is important for both sound and meaning. Young poets learn to be careful in their choice of words, maintaining the rhythmic music of language and enhancing the poem's message. Writing enhances the discovery of language and the discovery of self. The words in a poem have been chosen not only to communicate to an outside audience but also to clarify the inside perceptions of young writers about themselves.

The Lessons

Who benefits from these lessons?

These lessons have evolved from twenty years of teaching literacy to second through fifth graders at a multicultural magnet school. Ten ethnicities were represented throughout all the grades and each grade had a Spanish bilingual class. As well, children with a spectrum of special needs were included in all classrooms. Those children challenged by the reading and writing of the English language, were often more comfortable with the reading and writing of the genre of poetry. Reluctant readers can confidently read poetry's shorter passages because of the rhyming, repetition and more predictable text. Writer phobic students find that fewer words, as well as the informal demands on grammar and punctuation, make the writing process less daunting. At the same time this book of lessons will expand a love of the English language for those students who are further along their path of **word awareness development**.

Pedagogy

The pedagogies used in these lessons combine a *constructivist* philosophy with a more direct *explicit* instructional philosophy. To advance the development of word awareness, a child needs explicit instruction from a teacher. As this knowledge is assimilated, it serves to scaffold new knowledge that students can construct on their own. This combined approach to instruction allows students to become agents of their own knowledge.

The Poetry Environment

- Successful **word awareness development** is enhanced through learning environments that accommodate both a constructivist and explicit methodology of instruction.
- Optimally, several shelves of multicultural children's poetry books are accessible along with CDs with poets reading poetry.
- Poetic language is imaginative, creative, and fresh, occurring not only in poetry, but in all writing.
- If a child's **word awareness development** is continually nourished with poetry instruction, that child will speak poetically and apply it to all genres of writing. Children's words will mean what they say regardless of the genre.

How this Book Is Organized

The ultimate goal of this book is to inspire a lifetime curiosity for words and an appreciation for their complexity and significance. Everyone has a story to tell. It is heard when one has the "right" words to tell it. Words are the most basic tools for a writer. It is a teacher's responsibility to hone their students' word awareness development.

Children need words to interpret who and why they are. Interpreting the world is the gift of being human. When children can find the "just – right" words, they can order their entanglement of young emotions, not only for themselves but also for those who are listening to them. Word awareness development not only assists the developing young writer but as well the dedicated teacher. Both become lovers of language and master communicators.

Critical thinking about words occurs during the instruction of poetry. Because of its brevity the student can particularly focus on the sound, texture, and sensory impact of words as well as their significance. Also, the minimal nature of poetry makes the writing task less daunting. This allows young writers to become bolder and more practiced and competent in word use and intensify their word awareness development.

This book is organized in eight lessons of **word awareness development** with an addendum of teacher resources and inspiration.

All lessons note both the **explicit and implicit instruction** of four important poetic elements.

Poetic Elements

- The four important poetic elements addressed in these lessons are: **rhythm; heart and message; image and comparison; word choice.**
- The seeds of these elements are apparent in the very young before any formal instruction.
- **Rhythm** begins with babies' babble and their pleasure in melodious speech.
- **Heart and Message** emerges with children's desire to passionately communicate what is pertinent.
- **Image and Comparison** evolves from children's joy with the sensuous world and early ability to imagine the abstract through their concrete experience.
- **Word Choice** becomes important to children as they learn to discover their surroundings and share their ideas. A teacher's job is to cultivate a child's natural gift of verbal play and advance it to higher stages of word awareness and effective communication.

The Progression of the Lessons

These lessons progress from the basic to the advanced. They are listed in this manner in the table of contents. Trust your teacher intuition and use this book as a resource—a guiding light for word awareness development. Children have varying learning rates and styles. Trust the individual child's lead.

Lesson Instruction

- **The lessons are organized into sessions.** A teacher can spend one day on a session or stretch it out for a week or two, depending on class competency, interest, and available time.
- A child's agility with language and confidence with learning will grow with each session. If growth is not apparent, sessions need to be taught at a slower pace.
- Poetic language is imaginative, creative and fresh, occurring not only in poetry, but as well in all writing.
- The more practice students have with the elements of poetry, the more successful they will become in **word awareness development.**
- Sessions are best presented at a pace that allows for both teacher and student enjoyment of the lessons. A teacher's affection for poetry assures a student's affection for language.
- Lessons are more successful if teachers participate by writing their own poetry along with the students and **braving** the assignment.

Consistent Process

There is a consistent process to the instruction of the lessons meant to aid teachers to enter into a rhythm of learning. Not all the steps are used in every session, but all are used throughout every lesson.

- a) **WHY THIS LESSON:** Explains the overall objective of the lesson.
- b) **WHY THIS SESSION:** Explains the objective of each session.
- c) **SAY IT:** Is offered as suggested instructional script for the teacher.
- d) **SHOW IT:** References the resources and actions that a teacher uses to visually present the lesson, from mentor texts, videos, you tubes, or a teacher's modelling.
- e) **DISCOVER IT:** References the class's active engagement. This may involve partnering with classmates, exploring activity sheets, drawing, acting, etc.
- f) **NOTE IT:** In this step the teacher will use a smartboard or pens and paper to chart students' participation, progress, and learning discoveries. The noting can be used for comparing other work and/or for student reflection.

g) **BRAVE IT:** Students write their own creations from the inspired lessons. This does not happen in every session, for sometimes it takes several sessions for a child to muster the courage and confidence to venture out into a creation of his or her own.

h) **SHARE IT:** After students "brave it," they share. This sharing might happen in a writers' circle, or be pinned on a class corkboard, entered into a writing contest, or published in the school newsletter.

i) **CONTINUE IT:** Suggests ways that a teacher can continue the session, progress of the lessons, or the learning discoveries.

j) **NEW HABITS:** Suggests new practices to include in the classroom to make the environment more word-awareness friendly.

k) **EXAMPLES:** These are real examples from students who have completed a session or lesson.

Mentor Texts

Mentor texts are both authors' published work and students' original poetry that are used throughout these lessons. They are meant to serve as models and inspiration for both students and teachers. There are **required** and **suggested** purchases of mentor texts. Required texts are definitely needed because the session of instruction depends on the text. Other texts are suggested for purchase because they will enhance a particular lesson. Before beginning a two or three month instruction of lessons, be sure to look ahead and see which books you will need to order. Most often Amazon will have used, inexpensive copies of the **required** and **suggested** texts. A complete list of suggested and required texts is included at the back of this book.

Published Poems

The published poems in this book have been permitted by the publisher or author or are in the public domain. There are many other choices of poems that may be more appropriate for your class and grade level. These can be found in the **(R) Required** or **(S) Suggested** books in the bibliography.

It benefits the classroom teachers and their students to expand their homeroom libraries with quality poetry books and other word awareness development resources. Also, lessons are more impactful, by replacing or supplementing the poetry in *Word Choice Matters* with relevant poetic text for individual classrooms.

Activity Sheets

Lesson/session-specific Activity Sheets are provided at the end of each lesson. These can be photocopied for use by the children. Activity Sheets can also be downloaded as printable PDFs from: poetrylost.wordpress.com

PLEASE NOTE:

✦ Lessons are always more successful if teachers participate by writing their own poetry along with the students and **braving** the assignment.

✦ Activity sheets can be downloaded as PDFs from: **poetrylost.wordpress.com**

✦ Lesson 1: Beginning Rhythm

Explicit **Poetic Element Instruction:** Beginning Rhythm
Implied **Poetic Element Learning:** Choosing the Right Word; Image and Comparison; Heart

WHY THIS LESSON:

Rhythm is the most basic element of language. Early in life children enjoy manipulating sounds in a rhythmic manner. By 10 months they are engaging in multisyllabic utterances and reduplicated babble. Their experimentation with sound is delicious. All this is a precursor to a child's delight in the rhythms and intonations found in nursery rhymes and other simple rhyming. It is an organic relationship as rhythm is always coursing in and through a young child's body. Effective writers pay attention to the rhythm of their words as well as the message.

Session 1: RHYTHM MAESTRO

Materials needed:
- *Chart paper or smart board*
- **Poem Packet for Rhythm** *for each student (Check this packet for your students' level. If not appropriate use your own poetry choices.)*
- *Baton or ruler*

Note: Bold *items on the materials list are activity sheets that are provided at the end of each lesson.*

WHY THIS SESSION

Students begin to connect words with music. They discover this rhythm in words through poetry. Just like music, poetry has rhythm and can be conducted as a conductor or maestro would lead an orchestra. The way that one reads a poem can give it different interpretations. Awareness of the relationship between sound and meaning encourages word play.

SAY IT

Today begins our study of words. By the end of our study, you will love words, hug words, dance with words. Kind of silly to think that you go over to a word and you say, "Hey would you like to dance?" and then you listen to the music and begin to do the dance. Pretty fun, though. We are going to use poetry to get to know and love words. When I read a poem I can hear the rhythm. I can hear when the poem should be read soft or loud or fast or slow. I can direct the reading of a poem like the leader of a band conducts instruments to be played soft or loud or fast or slow. Not only can you conduct it like a song, but you can hear the rhythm and dance to the words. Now we are going to do all of that with this **Poem Packet for Rhythm** that I am passing out.

SHOW IT

- Read the first poem aloud. Be dramatic in the rise and fall of your voice.
- Then take a ruler and direct your reading as if you were leading an orchestra. Continue to be dramatic in the rise and fall of your voice as well as with your baton movements.
- Now conduct the children reading the poem aloud together, using loud, soft, fast, and slow voices.
- Be as dramatic and clear with the swing of the baton as possible.

DISCOVER IT

- Ask for a volunteer to take a turn conducting the same poem. As before, classmates will follow the directions of the baton and read the poem aloud.
- No rhythm direction is right or wrong.
- Encourage different interpretations by giving several children a turn with the baton.
- Notice with the children how lines or words that one child may interpret as strong and slow may be expressed by another child as soft and fast.
- Notice too, how interesting it is that words and ideas can have more than one meaning or interpretation.

NOTE IT

- After each student reads and interprets the poem, chart volunteered reasons why students liked their fellow classmate's poetry interpretation.
- Ask the students and then the "maestro" why they think those choices were made.

CONTINUE IT

- Read over the rest of the poems in the packet in chorus, choosing students to conduct them. Most importantly, encourage students to notice the rhythm in their language.
- Have students bring in their own poems from home or ones chosen at independent reading or library time, and conduct these.

NEW HABITS

- Read a poem each day at the beginning of your teaching session.
- There is no discussion, just pure enjoyment.
- Copy the poems that you read to create an easily accessible collection.
- Encourage students to read and share the poems at independent reading.

Session 2: RHYTHM PERFORMER

Materials needed:
- **Performance Steps** *activity sheets*
- *A class chart of the Performance Steps*
- *A prepared "poetry music sheet" of two lines from one of the poems in the poem packet for class viewing. Indicate your interpretation for reading the poem aloud (see Activity Sheet **Performance Steps**, on page 24), e.g. use parentheses around the words you want to say softly; highlight the words you want to say loudly; put a wavy line where you want to speak slowly; and a dotted line under the words you want to say quickly. Unmarked words are spoken in a regular voice.*
- **Poem Packet for Rhythm** *activity sheets*

WHY THIS SESSION

This session is an exercise of naming something that you cannot see. The students will practice naming the rhythm that they feel, as well as acting out that rhythm. This exercise will assist in establishing a rhythm of language in all genres of writing.

SAY IT

Today we will start dancing with words. We will use the rhythm in the words of the poems that we have been "Maestro-ing." I will appoint teams and one poem from the packet that you will perform for the class. Performance will consist of these steps that are on the performance chart. *(Pass out the* **Performance Steps** *activity sheet and reference the large chart that you have made.)* You will make your poem into a music sheet by noting which words you want to say quickly, slowly, loudly, and softly. Then, you will make a dance or movements that go along with your poem. Decide how you can act out or move to some of the ideas in your poem. I will do one line of poetry for you to give you an example. One person can read while the other(s) act(s). Each group will read their poem and dance it for the whole class.

SHOW IT

- Prepare two lines of poetry, noting the strong and fast, soft or slow parts on chart paper to serve as a model for the students.
- Read the poem from your "music sheet" following the notations and then dramatize it with gesture, mime and free movement.
- Encourage the students to be creative in their dramatic interpretations.

DISCOVER IT

- As each group performs their song and dance, ask the class for words that describe the rhythm that the performers have chosen, *e.g. quick, bumpy, galloping, stumbly, etc.* Allow words of their own creation.
- Help them be creative with their descriptors to extend the students' vocabulary and further challenge them to name the abstract.

NOTE IT

- Create a chart that includes all the suggested words that have been offered by the class to describe the enacted poems.
- Encourage awareness of the varied movements and rhythm possibilities in each poem.

CONTINUE IT

- Have the students choose poems that they like and create poetry "music sheets."
- At morning meetings, or transitional moments, give the children opportunities to present their creations.

Session 3: WALKING RHYTHM MACHINES

Materials needed:
- *Paper*
- *Pencil*
- *Drawing paper*
- *Crayons*
- **Rhythm Choice & Sound & Movement** *activity sheet*
- **Examples of Rhythm Choices** *activity sheet*

WHY THIS SESSION

Students will discover that rhythm is all around us. We **MAKE** rhythm. We **ARE** rhythm. We use words to express rhythmic experience.

SAY IT

Rhythm is very comfortable to us. It is happening all around us. It is happening inside us and outside us. We are rhythm machines. What is the rhythm that is inside of us? Be very quiet and listen and look around our circle. What natural rhythms do you see and hear?

SHOW IT

- When everyone is quiet, dramatize the inhale and exhale of your breath.
- Ask the students to raise their hands as they notice you dramatizing natural rhythms such as, eye blinking, heartbeat, swallowing, finger tapping.
- Ask them to name the rhythms they noticed.
- Point out that we are veritable rhythm machines.

DISCOVER IT

- Once the students have identified the rhythms that are connected to their bodies, explain that you are going to begin to recognize the rhythm beyond their bodies.
- Pass out the **Rhythm Choice & Sound & Movement** activity sheet and the **Examples of Rhythm Choices** activity sheet.
- Have them return to their desks so they have a hard surface to write on to eventually fill in the **Rhythm Choice & Sound & Movement** activity sheet.
- Together read the list of **Examples of Rhythm Choices** activity sheet.
- Stop at some of the examples and point out how the example shows a ***regular repeated pattern of sound or movement***. Emphasize that this repeated pattern is rhythm.
- Tape this definition on the board or wall for this lesson so it can be referred to and understood.

- Model the rhythmic sound and movement some of the examples manifest. e.g. If it is a basket ball, the words used to explain the rhythmic sound might be *palunk, palunk, palunk.*
- If it is a leaf floating to the ground, the words used to express the rhythmic movement might be *slowly back, slowly forth, slowly back , slowly forth.*
- If it is a carrot being chomped, the words used to explain the rhythmic sound might be *chomp, crunch, chomp, crunch.*
- Hand out the **Rhythm Choice & Sound & Movement** activity sheet that has two examples of rhythm choices modeled.
- Using the examples from the **Examples of Rhythm Choices** activity sheet or their own created examples have them try to fill in the **Rhythm Choice & Sound & Movement** activity sheet.
- Encourage the students to be creative and reach deeply into their minds for the "right" words to express the rhythm.
- Have them choose their favorite one and illustrate it.

NOTE IT

- When the students have finished their list and drawn their picture, have them share their illustration and their rhythm example with expressed rhythm and sound.
- Chart the ideas that have been suggested by the students.
- These will be used for titles or first lines for simple rhythm poems.

BRAVE IT

- Point out to the children that they have some very good first lines of poems on their **Rhythm Choice & Sound & Movement** activity sheet.
- They will now take one of the lines and try to create a poem. This is the dance with words that they had been told would happen.
- A simple model can be suggested by the teacher

Carrots crunch,

crunch

crunch

in my mouth

becoming

little orange chunks

to swallow

swallow

guu...ulp.

SHARE IT

- Have the students share any efforts of poetry that they have created.
- Have them speak it with the rhythm that they think is appropriate for their poem.
- Type up some of the poems for display.

- Begin to give their poems line breaks to give the students the idea of the appearance of a poem.

CONTINUE IT

- Have the students continue to bring in noticed rhythmic happenings.
- Together, as a class or as individuals, create class poems from the chart created from **note it.** These can be similar to the poems that the children created when they **braved it**.

NEW HABITS

- With the poems you are reading daily, point out the rhythm and have students describe it.
- Choose non-rhyming as well as rhyming poems.

Session 4: RHYTHM IN OUR WORLD

Materials needed:
- *Chart Paper with two columns marked as:* 1) Rhythm Choice, and 2) Show Don't Tell
- **Rhythm Choice & Show Don't Tell Model** *activity sheet*
- **Rhythm Choice & Show Don't Tell** *activity sheet*

WHY THIS SESSION

Through realizing that the possibilities of rhythm are everywhere, the students will become more attuned to the rhythm of life. They begin to use comparisons to communicate their observations.

SAY IT

Now we are going to look at the rhythm that is outside of this building. We are going to take a rhythm walk. Some of the things that are on our chart from last session may be things that we hear or see or feel on our rhythm walk. The only rhythm that I do not want to hear is the rhythm of your voices. We have to be absolutely quiet so we can notice all the other rhythms around us. If you see something that has rhythm, point to it, but do not say a word. When we come back we will remember what we saw, heard and felt that was rhythmic.

SHOW IT

As you walk with the children outside, point, but do not speak, to possibilities of rhythm. For example:
- Point to the *swish of shoes* passing through leaves piled on the sidewalk.
- Point to a *bouncing ball* in a playground.

- Point to a *church bell ringing*.
- Be as imaginative as you would like your students to be.

DISCOVER IT

- When the students return, have them get into pairs and share their discoveries of the outside world, discussing their sound and movement observations.

NOTE IT

- Have the students return to the circle and share some of their examples
- Before they share pass out the **Rhythm Choice & Show Don't Tell Model** activity sheet. Explain that you just don't want them to tell you what they heard or saw, you want them to really show you. The best way to do this is through a comparison. Refer to your examples on the **Rhythm Choice & Show Don't Tell Model** activity sheet.
- As the students share, note their **Rhythm Choices** on the prepared chart and together try to create comparisons to help the audience better understand what rhythm was experienced.
- Encourage *all* students to "have a go" at it. The students should be confident in their understanding of rhythm when they return to their seats to complete it on their own.

BRAVE IT

- Hand out the **Rhythm Choice & Show Don't Tell** activity sheet. These they will fill in on their own.
- They should not be in pairs as they have had enough experience to try independently to create the comparative descriptions.

SHARE IT

- Return to the circle and have the students share their worksheets.
- Continue to note these shared **Rhythm Choices & Show Don't Tell,** on the class chart.
- The results of this chart will inspire the next session's writing.

CONTINUE IT

- Continue to encourage this process of noticing and comparing as a fun play with words and sounds.
- You are not telling them HOW to use alliteration, repetition, metaphor, personification, onomatopoeia or other poetry strategies. They will use it naturally. If you hear it being used, you can note it.
- Explicit instruction of these poetry strategies will occur in later lessons, but the vocabulary can begin to be familiar.

NEW HABITS

- When children go out to recess or take a field trip, ask them to notice the rhythms of their environment.
- When they report on what they noticed, encourage them to compare it to something that helps the audience to better understand the experience that the observer had.

EXAMPLES

Below are examples of "show don't tell" phrases students suggested after experiencing a rhythm walk:

- Car engines purr like kittens. (Point out importance of comparisons and note it is a simile.)
- Church bells tap like pieces of metal. (Point out simile.)
- Church bells are like waves of sound. (Point out simile.)
- The car engine snores. (Point out it is like a person and is called personification.)
- Clitter clatter, clitter clatter of the wheels. (Point out that this is called onomatopoeia.)
- Cars move like a rolling wave. (Point out simile.)
- Church bells bong and pounce into us like lions. (Point out simile.)
- Zoom, zoom, zing, the cars rumble along. (Point out the alliteration.)
- Wind wags blades of grass. (Point out the alliteration.)
- Branches wave and twist. (Point out personification.)
- Birds flap their wings like flags. (Point out simile.)
- Wind whooshes and whirls around like a crazy dance. (Point out the alliteration.)

Session 5: RHYTHM WRITERS

Materials needed:
- *Chart of Rhythm Choices & Sound & Movement Phrases created from the Session 3*
- *Completed* **Rhythm Choice & Show Don't Tell** *activity sheet from Session 4*
- *Paper and pencils for each student*
- *An adult for each group of 3-7 children (this is a beginning effort of the students' poetry and will need a supporting adult)*

WHY THIS SESSION

The children will *be bold and dare* to create their own poems. It is important to keep this effort fun, as these beginning efforts of writing and word exploration must feel successful to the student.

SAY IT

Today I know you are ready to create your own poems. We are going to use our completed **Rhythm Choice & Show Don't Tell** activity sheets and ideas from the class chart as inspiration for these poems. We will get into small groups with an adult leading each group.

SHOW IT and DISCOVER IT

- The creation of the poems is best modeled in small groups. Therefore, the best time to present this lesson is during guided reading, small group work, or other times that adult help is available.

- In the small group the teacher scaffolds the children's writing efforts by adding suggestions of repetition, alliteration, simile, and personification along with the phrases that they already have created.
- As the students observe this modeling, they will become more independently adept.
- The following are poems that were created by three small groups of students and an adult.

POEM 1

In the first poem, the teacher led the students to compare how sound waves were like ocean waves. They then made the connection of beaches and bells. They have made a concrete connection of a sound wave feeling like a water wave. Once they had done this, their imaginations carried them to the image of the beach and combined it with the rhythmic ringing of the church bell.

BING BONG Beaches

Bing, bong
Bing, bong
Waves of sound roll over us
Like tides on a beach
Smoothing away
The day's roughness
Bing, bong
Bing, bong
The roughness of sand
Returning it again
Smooth and wet
Bing, bong
Bing, bong
When I step
On wet sand
A trail of
Watery footprints
Follow me
Bing, bong
Bing, bong

POEM 2

In the next class poem, ideas from four phrases concerning wind were discussed. An image was proposed for the first line of the poem and the other five students continued the image. The teacher helped to change the sentence "the smooth waving wind was waving blades of grass" to a poetry phrase like "smooth waving wind wags blades of grass." Or helped them to change "the leaves look like green flags waving" to "leaves flag greenness." Modeling this kind of experimentation with language inspires a child to be equally adventurous. The wind is always a great subject for young writers, as it is familiar and easily compared. No one can really see it but its results are very concrete. It can easily be used as personification of nature. The child's imagination can be "blown away."

Smooth Waving Wind

Smooth waving wind wags blades of grass
From side to side
Branches twist
Leaves flag greenness
New life
In the air
Air brings its wind
To another place
Birds wings flapping
Like a flag
In the clean warm wind.

POEM 3

The children in this last group, also chose wind as their topic and their title. They then listed all their personal images of the effects of wind.

The Wind

The Woosh of the wind
whips along
the road
blowing hair
tugging coats open
and wrapping us
with cold air.
Wind whooshing and whirring
around the sky
blowing the tree's leaves
and seeds
off of them
pushing seagulls out of sight.

NOTE IT

- Share the poems in a group circle and note why the other students like the poems. Encourage them to see the rhythm in the words.
- Ask them what they see when they close their eyes and listen to the poem.
- Encourage students to use comparisons by drawing mind pictures with the words they use to discuss the poems.

BRAVE IT

- The children are ready to write their own poems.
- Encourage the children to go back to the chart of phrases and the class-created poems for titles and ideas.
- Encourage them to play with repeating words and sounds in their poems.

SHARE IT

- Share all poems, whether they are two lines or many lines, in a writing circle.
- Continue to add to the chart from the earlier group poems about why the students like the poems. This serves as a structure for group discussion.
- Observe and emphasize rhythm and images created by the words.

CONTINUE IT

- The chart of phrases can become part of the print on the wall for several weeks.
- Students who finish work early can continue to create poetry and engage in word play, using the chart of communal rhythm and sound ideas.

NEW HABITS

- When reading any text, note poetic language and how it draws our attention.

EXAMPLES

Following are results of some second grade students' efforts with this lesson.

The Storm

The blunder, slunder of the storm
as it blows hard through the trees wildly
the day is dark as black
all day long.

The slunder, dunder of the storm
the thunder as it rolls past my eyes
the blunder slunder of the storm
as the rain cries past my eyes.
The trees have a flit, blit
shaking and throwing leaves
as it is
a black day on Monday.

Melissa, 2nd grade

Rain

P-lip p-lop plippty p-lop
blup
a
rain
drop
bounces off
an umbrella
plop on the cement it goes.

Lia, 2nd grade

The following poems were written by more advanced writers who had once experienced this first lesson and had continued **boldly** to expand on and **deeply** explore the rhythm in their words.

Little Mouse

Tsk, tsk, tsk
of a tiny
mouse
was greeting
his mouslings
in the alley
hissity, hiss, hiss
hisses the alley cat
trying to catch
his prey.

Mary, 3rd grade

The Snake

The snake
slithering
silently along the rough forest floor
sees a mouse skimmering along
and the snake just now
realizing
his hunger
and then
CRUNCH
the mouse disappears
and the snake
slides
into the underbrush.

                    Ethan, 4th grade

Chickens

A flap and a flutter
while he heads to the roof

the black hen stands proud
and tall
while looking at the sun.

a whoosh and a wup
while another one goes up.

A flash and a flutter
while he heads to the roof

while he heads to the roof
A flap and a flutter

                    Noah, 3rd grade

Rubber band

Literacy fades away
as the bending
twisting maze of rubber band
entwines my fingers
as it pulls me
from the real world.

I plummet deeper into my thoughts
of candy cane forests and peppermint stepping stones
of cotton candy and Hershey's kisses hail.

Kora
my name echoes in meaningless reality,
Kora
I somehow float to the surface
of the real world from the depths of
my thoughts.

My eyes snap open
I look around the empty classroom.
Mary is standing in the doorway
saying
"Kora, everyone has gone to lunch!"

Kora, 5th grade

Spring Wind

Smooth spring wind
wags blades of grass
from side to side.
Branches twist.
Leaves flag greenness.
New Life
fills the air
that brings wind
to another place.
Birds' wings flap as they
glide
gracefully
on the warm wind.

3rd grade group poem

A Child's Thought

At seven, when I go to bed
I find such pictures, in my head
Castles with dragons prowling around
Gardens where magic fruits are found
Fair ladies prisoned in a tower
Or lost in an enchanted bower.*
While gallant horsemen ride by streams
That border all this land of dreams
I find so clearly in my head
At seven, when I go to bed.

Robert Louis Stevenson

a shelter in a garden made with tree branches

Chickens

A flap and a flutter
while he heads to the roof

The black hen stands proud
and tall
while looking at the sun

A woosh and a wup
while another one goes up

A flash and a flutter
while he heads to the roof

while he heads to the roof
a flap and a flutter.

Noah 3rd grade

LESSON 1: ACTIVITY SHEET   19

The Bully

Bobby Nelson is the toughest kid in the class
I am the smallest.
His hoarse voice finds me every day
on the way to schoool and home again.
"Hey rabbit, whatcha doin' ?
A rock drops into my gut.
He walks next to me,
throws his elbow into my ribs and edges me to the curb
hoping I will take a swing at him.
I tried once and he flipped
me like a toy dog.

One day Jim, my best friend, gets fed up
with Nelson's jabs and taunts
Someone on the playground yells, "fight"
and a ring of kids surrounds them.
"Hit 'im, Jim."
"Take him, Nelson."
saying , "Yeah, yeah, yeah,
think you're big
think you're tough."
Nelson takes a swing;
Jim catches his arm
and twists him to the ground;
the dust flies, the circle cheers.
Jim sits on Nelson
like we own the playground,
the school and everything in it.

Donald Graves

POETRY

Poetry is like some
sugar-crazed teenager
who just got a license
but refuses to follow
the rules of the road.

It races out of control
then jams up the traffic by
going reeeeeaaaalll slooooooooooow.
It turns up the music so loud
you can't sleep at night.
I can't figure out how it Decides
to capitalize certain Words
Punctuation ? Ha! A joke!
Won't use complete sentences

And why does it refuse to
     stay
          on
               the
                    line?
The most annoying thing?
Poetry won't shut up.
It embarrasses everyone
by telling the truth.
                    Ralph Fletcher

DREAMS

To fling my arms wide
In some place in the sun
To whirl and to dance
Till the white day is done.
Then rest at cool evening
Beneath a tall tree
While night comes on gently
    Dark like me-
That is my dream!

To fling my arms wide
In the face of the sun
Dance! Whirl! Whirl!
Till the quick day is done
Rest at pale evening......
A tall slim tree.....
Night come tenderly
Black like me.

        Langston Hughes

Rubber band

Literacy fades away
as the bending
twisting maze of rubber band
entwines my fingers
as it pulls me
from the real world.

I plummet deeper into my thoughts
of candy cane forests and peppermint stepping stones
of cotton candy and Hersey's kisses hail.

Kora
my name echoes in meaningless reality,
Kora
I somehow float to the surface
of the real world from the depths of
my thoughts.

My eyes snap open
I look around the empty classroom.
Mary is standing in the doorway
saying
"Kora, everyone has gone to lunch!"

Kora, 4th grade

Name _____

Performance steps

Make a poetry music sheet:

- Use parentheses around words you want to say **softly**.

- Highlight the words you want to say **loudly**.

- Put a wavy line under the words you want to say **slowly**.

- Put a dotted line under the words you want to say **quickly**.

Moving to the words:

- Choose movements you will use to show the poem.

- Practice reading your poetry song sheet while you make your poetic moves.

- Decide who will read and who will move to perform the poem for the class.

WORDS ON FIRE, © 2017, Heidi Simmons

Name _____

Examples of Rhythm Choices

1. basketball bouncing
2. car tires rolling
3. car horn beeping
4. wind in the trees
5. breaking sticks
6. yelling children
7. sap dribbling
8. birds wings flapping
9. leaves floating in the wind
10. laughing children
11. hugging
12. shivering
13. rhythm of imagination
14. rhythm of a dream
15. train chugging
16. brushing teeth
17. chomping carrots

Name _____

RHYTHM CHOICE	REPEATED PATTERN OF SOUND OR MOVEMENT
Chomping a carrot	*Chomp, crunch, chomp, crunch, chomp crunch*
Leaf floating to the ground	*Slowly back, slowly forth, slowly back, slowly forth*

Name _____

RHYTHM CHOICE	SHOW DON'T TELL
	1. the sound it makes 2. a comparison 3. what it does
Squishing mud	1. slip, slop, squish 2.&3. squirting up between toes like a little fountain of mud
Puddle rippling with the wind	2.&3. puddle circles hold hands and dance round and round in the wind
Velcro pulling apart	1. kashish, kashish, kashish 2.&3. clinging friends are ripped apart
Shoes scuffing on pavement	1. swish, swoosh, swish, swoosh 2. Like sandpaper rubbing a rough board 3. no steps just gliding

Name _____

RHYTHM CHOICE	SHOW DON'T TELL 1. the sound it makes 2. a comparison 3. what it does

✦ Lesson 2: Beginning Heart and Message

Explicit **Poetic Element Instruction:** Beginning Heart and Message
Implied **Poetic Element Learning**: Choosing The Right Word; Rhythm; Image and Comparison

WHY THIS LESSON

Writing can give students an opportunity to use words to share feelings and communicate their experiences and observations. A child builds up a resource of words and then depending on opportunity and need, uses language resources for self-expression. Through thoughtful and imaginative use of words, the child gives words depth with applicable importance.

Below, a fifth grade student expresses her heartfelt feelings and creative ideas about imagination in her poem *Imagina-Flower*. With unique language she has communicated a concept of imagination that has satisfied her inner self and entertained an outside reader.

The Imagina-Flower

Like a flower imagination
is planted permanently as
a seed in your
dirt – mind.
The idea sprouts growing a strong thought stem.
Budding and flowering
as new ideas are formed
added to the strong
tall standing
growing
imaginaflower.

Meg, 5th grade

Session 1: HEART AND MESSAGE DETECTIVES

Materials needed:
- *Copies of activity sheet* **Writing Needs Heart**
- *Paper and pencil*
- *Chart with the two questions from* **SAY IT**

WHY THIS SESSION

The students will notice that in good writing words are used where there is apparent feeling and communication of a heartfelt message. It is not only in poetry that language can be so impactful; all texts are more effective when written with poignant language and emotion. Students will learn how to use language that creates clear images, awakens the imagination and is thoughtful and heartfelt.

SAY IT

You have been brilliant with your discovery of rhythm all around you and creating rhythmic language. Now we are going to figure out how our writing is not only rhythmic but heartfelt. Perhaps imagining a writing with a heart is a silly image. But if your writing does not have heart, it will not be interesting to you the writer and therefore not interesting to your reader.
So (*and point to the chart*) **1) When does a heartfelt idea happen? 2) How can we share it with our reader?**

As we understood rhythm in writing by studying poetry, we will study heart in writing through poetry. In the poem that I pass out to you there are answers to the chart questions. [Pass out **Writing Needs Heart.**]
I will place you in pairs and then together you can be good detectives and discover the answers to these two questions.

SHOW IT

- Gather the students in a writing circle.
- After the students have received copies of the poem, slowly read it aloud.
- Have the class read it a second time together, and encourage them to think about the questions that have been written on the chart paper.

DISCOVER IT

- Ask the children to turn to a fellow student beside them in their writing circle.
- With this partner have them discuss 1) Why they think that the students in the second stanza of the poem, thought that the image of "a poem with a

heart" was silly? and 2) what they think the answers are to the two charted questions.

NOTE IT

- Note their suggested answers below the charted two questions.
- Encourage the students to answer the questions in general for example 1) that a heartfelt idea derives from an experience with someone or something that they care about and love. It can be a person, a sport, a food, an animal, an experience, and 2) the best way to communicate the heartfelt idea to the reader is to make a picture in the reader's mind. For example when the poem talks about the snow falling hard, it is compared to a curtain of white.
- In the next session the students will become more specific about the answers

NEW HABITS

- While doing a read aloud or while leading a reading group, point out text where the author uses language to express heartfelt ideas.

Session 2: HEART AND MESSAGE LENS

Materials needed:
- *Prepare a class chart titled: LENS QUESTIONS: HOW DO WE KNOW THERE IS HEART. Make two columns labeled: 1)* **When** *did the important heartfelt idea happen? 2)* **What** *did it look like using a comparison?*
- **Lens Questions: How Do We Know There Is Heart** *activity sheet*
- **Writing Needs Heart** *activity sheet*

WHY THIS SESSION:

In this session the children will learn to use the "lens questions" for recognizing text that is 1) heartfelt and 2) successfully communicated by using comparisons to create thoughtful, clear images.

SAY IT

We have looked at a poem and seen how language creates thoughtful, clear images that help us to feel deeply, awakening our imaginations and our hearts. We can use a special lens that you can look through to see if *your* writing creates thoughtful, clear images that help your readers to feel deeply. The lens you will use is a lens of two questions: 1) **When** does the writer show an important idea? 2) **What** is it like using a comparison?

When writers share a moment that is important, their language is thoughtful, imaginative and heartfelt. Let's look at the poem **Writing Needs Heart** again poem and use this question lens, to discover how her language shows that the idea is important and heartfelt.

SHOW IT

- With the students, look at the poem **Writing Needs Heart** using the class prepared chart of LENS QUESTIONS.
- **When** is a time, that Heidi has an important heartfelt idea? **When** "the snow falls hard outside."
- And 2) **What** is it like? She **compares** it to a curtain of white. She creates a clear, thoughtful image of a snow storm where the snow is coming down so hard it looks like a white curtain has been pulled across the window.
- Again, she shares a time when she has a heartfelt idea 1) "when the moon is bright" and 2) shares what it looks like to a halo. (A halo is what angels have over their heads. Perhaps she is saying that the moon is like an angel to her. Good comparisons can give the reader many possibile thoughts.)
- With partners, students will continue to explore the poem, **Writing Needs Heart**, look through their lens questions and answer 1) **when** does Heidi have a heartfelt idea and 2) **what** does it look like.

DISCOVER IT

- Pass out the activity sheet **Lens Questions: How Do We Know There Is Heart**.
- Grouping the students in pairs or teams, have them complete the activity sheet.

NOTE IT

- Ask the students to return to their writing circle to share their discoveries.
- Add the answers to the chart with the two observations already noted.
- As you read over the responses with the class, ask whether or not the students think that Heidi is writing about things that she knows well and can share with a thoughtful, clear image?
- Do they, the students, have new pictures in their head of a snow storm, a full moon, riding a bike, kittens purring, warm custard, and an ice cream cone ?
- One job of a writer is to help their readers see the world differently.

CONTINUE IT

- Find opportunities to point out excerpts that show the writer delivering thoughtful, clear, and strongly-felt images that help the students, see the world differently.

Session 3: CREATE YOUR HEART

Materials needed:
- *Heart shapes cut out for each child from 4x5 pieces of blank paper*
- *A model paper heart of the teacher's important heartfelt ideas*
- *A chart of the activity sheet* **Heartfelt Ideas**

WHY THIS SESSION

The students will be able to reflect on and write down, people, places, things, and happenings that are important and heartfelt in their lives.

SAY IT

We have seen how important heart is to writing. And we have learned to recognize it. Now we are going to think about the things in our own lives which we feel are important and heartfelt. We need to know these heartfelt ideas well enough that we can use language that communicates a thoughtful and strong-imaged message when we write about them.

I am going to give each student a paper heart. On these hearts I want you to write down something for which you have a heartfelt feeling. It may be a special person, a favorite place, a sport or activity, a particular outfit or toy, etc. Test if your idea is heartfelt by identifying **when** you had a particular heartfelt experience and **what** it looked like. Comparing it to something can help the reader to see your idea. For example, if you want to write about your mom, write "Mom" on the heart and then THINK **when** you have had an especially heartfelt feeling with her. It may be when she is reading to you. Then think of a comparison so we can feel the experience too. Perhaps you say, "I curl up **like a caterpillar** warm and soft in her lap."

SHOW IT

- Model a heart using the example of your own mom as a choice of an important idea to write about.
- Write "Mom" on a model heart.
- Turn to the charted activity sheet, **Heartfelt Ideas** and model filling it out.
- EXAMPLE: In the **when question** blank, put "when she reads to me."
- In the **what comparison**, put "I am like a caterpillar curled up in her lap."

BRAVE IT

- In pairs, ask the students to fill in their hearts with five to ten ideas.
- Instruct that when they have about five ideas, to share them with their partner and explain **when** the idea on the heart was particularly heartfelt and **what** it was like using a comparison.

SHARE IT

- Ask the students to return to the circle to share the ideas that they have written on their hearts.
- List these on a chart so other children may begin to get new ideas for their hearts.

CONTINUE IT

- Ask the children at morning meeting if they have experienced any heartfelt experiences the night before. Encourage them to write them down on their hearts as they can use the ideas for later poems.

Session 4: CREATE A HEART

Materials needed:
- *Heart shapes filled out with students' heartfelt ideas*
- **Heartfelt Ideas** *activity sheet*
- *Chart started in Session 3*

WHY THIS SESSION

In this session students will continue to explore their heartfelt ideas and will practice expanding their ideas into poems, using the "lens questions."

SAY IT

Today we are going to fill out the activity sheets that I modeled last session. Choose one of the ideas from your heart. Remember that you want to explain SPECIFICALLY, **when** you feel strongly about the idea and **what** it is like at that moment as described through a **comparison.**

If I were using my sister as an example, I might say it is **when** she braids my hair, and then describe **what** her hands are like: They are careful like a doctor's hands and never pull or tug.

SHOW IT

- Pass out **Heartfelt Ideas.**
- Refer back to the modeling that was done in the previous session with "Mom."
- Show how to insert your idea about a hair-braiding sister as they follow along with their activity sheets.

DISCOVER IT

- Send the students off to fill out their activity sheets. About ten minutes into this activity, have students share what they have accomplished so far.
- Their accomplishments may inspire other children who may be feeling stuck.

NOTE IT

- Ask the students to return to the circle with their paper hearts and activity sheets in hand.
- Chart the shared ideas on the prepared chart.
- When you have finished with the sharing, go back over the created class chart and ask if any students have connections with any of the ideas suggested from other students.
- Encourage them to take a minute to add ideas to their own hearts for later writing.

CONTINUE IT

- Have the students draw detailed pictures of their heartfelt moments **before beginning the next session** when they will write their own poems.
- At the beginning of morning meeting, ask if any students have any heartfelt moment to share that they have had the previous day or morning. This will help them to begin to notice moments in their lives for future use.

Session 5: BECOMING HEARTFELT WRITERS

Materials needed:

- *Paper and pencil*
- *Pictures students have created about their heartfelt ideas (if assigned)*
- *A prepared chart with the three ideas listed below in* **SAY IT**
- *Their completed activity sheets on* **Heartfelt Ideas.**

WHY THIS SESSION

The students will experience writing their own heartfelt pieces of writing, by using language that creates thoughtful, clear images that help readers feel deeply, awakening imagination and heart. They will begin to understand that all writing needs heart in it to be convincing and interesting.

SAY IT

Today, you will be the creators of heartfelt writing. You have all the tools for it to be fun and easy. You need to take out your completed **Heartfelt Ideas** activity sheet and use it to help you create poems that tell: **1)** the heartfelt idea; **2)** when you experience the heartfelt idea; and **3)** what it is like by using a comparison. I will model for you what I mean.

SHOW IT

Show the example of writing about the sister that was noted on my heart. I would write:

I see it in my sister
when she is braiding my hair
her fingers never tug, she weaves my braids loose, sometimes with flowers.

BRAVE IT

- Give the children their **Heartfelt Ideas** activity sheets.
- They may share quietly with a classmate when they finish an idea.

SHARE IT

- The students return to the circle and share as much as they have written.
- Encourage classmates to comment on what they particularly like.
- At the end of the sharing, give students time to voice what was a challenge to them, as well as what was fun for them.

CONTINUE IT

- Encourage students to find an opportunity before the next session to work further on their own couplets.
- OR begin to write new ones.

NEW HABITS

- When students are explaining or sharing something, encourage them to compare it to something that will help the listener or reader better visualize what they are trying to communicate.

EXAMPLES

I find heart in my family
when they are kissing me
their soft lips touching me makes me feel good.

Quinn, 2nd grade

I find heart in surfing
when I am in the curl of the wave
I look all the way down the tube of the water.

AJ, 2nd grade

I find heart in coloring
when I create a picture
I can see the picture pop out of the paper,
dancing, jumping and singing.

Kenya, 2nd grade

I find heart in a violin
when I hold the strings
my hand dances and twirls as I move
the bow back and forth

Anika, 2nd grade

I find heart in Dad
kissing me when I get hurt
he carefully places a bandaid on my knee
and whispers, "I love you, now come on let's play."

Camryn, 2nd grade

I find heart in my baby cousin
when he runs up to me
I hug him tight
admiring a big smile
I find heart in my mom
when she kisses me good night
Her soft lips make my
heart feel better
when I am having a bad day.
I find heart in my beta fish
when he swims around
the tank
a blur and a blend of
colors.

Zakar, 2nd grade

I find heart in the chickens' wings
when the chickens fly up to the roof
the wind blows
and I feel the wind from their wings
I find heart in rabbits
when their velvet fur touches my hand
and I look at their soft brown and white fur
I find heart in weaving
I get to the top of the loom
and my hand feels my work.

Noah, 2nd grade

Writing Needs Heart

The students gather and sit in their seat
The lesson is about to start
The teacher smiles, and folds her hands,
explains they will write with heart

Writing with a heart? The image is silly.
The students frown and look far away.
They dream of recess, where they can be free
and run around and just play.

She sees their scowls and knotted fists,
on each face a distant stare,
until she promises that their writing will reflect
that which they most care.

"When you really care, your writing has heart."
The children seem ready to listen.
Perhaps she had a special message
that the class had, in fact, been missin'

"I love," she says, "when the snow falls hard
and outside is a curtain of white
"I love," she says "when the moon is full
circled in a halo of light.

"I love," she says, "when I ride my bike
so fast the trees are a blur.
"I love," she says, "when my kitten sleeps
with a quiet rumbling purr.

"I love," she says, "when the custard is warm
and slip - slides into my tummy
"I love," she says, "when ice cream is coned."
Imprisoned in a bowl?....... It's not yummy.

The children are quiet and hear her words
"When you love, you show your heart
then create an image that your reader can see."
Ahhhhhh..... they get it!
        and their writing now can start.
                     Heidi Simmons

Name _____

Lens Questions: How Do We Know There Is Heart?

Using the Lens Questions:

    A) When does the poet show an important idea in the poem?

    B) What does it look like using a comparison?

When writers share an experience with heart, their language creates thoughtful, clear **images** that help readers feel deeply, by awakening the imagination and creating a heartfelt sense. Using the lens questions is a helpful way to find a poem's images and recognize a poem's heart.

We will start with the poem **Writing Needs Heart** and use the lens questions to find where her language in the poem creates images, and awakens heart.

- Look at each example from the poem.
- Use the lens questions.
- Write your ideas on the activity sheet for discussion.

EXAMPLES:

Q: When does the poet have a heartfelt idea?

A: When the snow falls hard

Q: What is it like?

A: A curtain of white

Q: When does the poet have a heartfelt idea?

A: When the moon is full.

Q: What is it like?

A: Circled in a halo of light.

Name _____

Look at the rest of the poem and complete these:

Q: When does the poet have a heartfelt idea?
A:_____

Q: What is it like?
A:_____

Q: When does the poet have a heartfelt idea?
A:_____

Q: What is it like?
A:_____

Q: When does the poet have a heartfelt idea?
A:_____

Q: What is it like?
A:_____

Q: When does the poet have a heartfelt idea?
A:_____

Q: What is it like?
A:_____

Name _____

WHEN does your important heartfelt idea happen?

Example: When my mother reads to me.

Heartfelt Idea: _____

_____

_____

_____

Heartfelt Idea: _____

_____

_____

_____

Heartfelt Idea: _____

_____

_____

_____

Heartfelt Idea: _____

_____

_____

_____

WHAT is it like using a comparison?

Example: I am like a caterpillar curled up on her lap.

Is Like: _____

_____

_____

_____

Is Like: _____

_____

_____

_____

Is Like: _____

_____

_____

_____

Is Like: _____

_____

_____

_____

✦ Lesson 3: Beginning Image and Comparison

Explicit **Poetic Element Instruction:** Beginning Image and Comparison
Implied **Poetic Element Learning**: Choosing the right word; Rhythm; Heart and Message

WHY THIS LESSON

A young child's sensory awareness is keener than an adult's, because children's primary means of receiving the world is through their five senses. They can perceive the world through sensory connections that reveal their individuality and create new perspectives for readers. For example, a child scoops her spoon into a puffy white dollop of whipped cream and then connects this to the cumulus clouds in an afternoon sky.

When a child conjures a comparative image, it not only satisfies a need to communicate but builds ***Image**-ination (IMAGINATION).* Creating impactful images is foundational to a child's success and pleasure in writing.

Session 1: BECOMING EXTRA SENSORY PERCEPTORS

Materials needed:
- **Spaghetti** *text*
- *Chart with the five senses listed across the top*
- *A chart with Questions asked in* **DISCOVER IT**

WHY THIS SESSION

The students will be introduced to the sensory power of words. They will understand that words can give a reader a virtual sensorial experience. When words are well chosen, the reader has a sense of actually hearing, tasting, smelling, seeing, or touching an experience that in reality is just some words on paper. The objective of this lesson is to encourage children to be aware of their five senses and find the words to awaken these senses in their readers.

SAY IT

Before we start this lesson today, help me list our five senses, which I will then chart. It is a writer's job to awaken these five senses through well-chosen words. A writer can describe an experience with words that make you (the reader) feel like you are right there tasting, seeing, hearing, touching, or smelling a description in the book. But how can words awaken our five senses? They don't smell or taste or make a noise. They don't feel like anything and they all look the same; just little squiggles on flat white paper. I am going to show you: If any of those five senses is dozing, I am about to wake them, and perk them right up!!!!

SHOW IT

- Tell the class to close their eyes and listen as **Spaghetti** is read aloud for a first time. Instruct the students that it is their job to notice which of their five senses are being awakened during the reading.
- Pass out copies of **Spaghetti**. Read it aloud for a second time, and have the students follow along, with a second chance of noticing where each of the five senses is "awakened."

DISCOVER IT:

- Place the children with partners and instruct that with each question they have a few seconds to confer and then volunteer an answer.
- Ask the charted questions aloud:
  a) Were you there with the spaghetti?
  b) What could you **taste** . . . (*possible answer*) the ball of pasta and tomato carefully wound on my fork
  c) What could you **smell** . . . (*possible answer*) the hot tomatoey aroma
  d) What could you **see** . . . (*possible answer*) me winding the spaghetti round and round my fork
  e) What could you **feel or touch**? . . . (*possible answer*) the hot plate and the cold smooth fork
  f) What could you **hear?** . . . (*possible answer*) me yell out "Owwwww!" with pain

NOTE IT

- As the students respond, chart their responses under the five sense categories. Point out at the end of their sharing that a plate of spaghetti was not even present and they had all these sensual experiences. This is the power of words!!

BRAVE IT

- Ask the students to think of favorite foods.
- Write the suggestions on the chart paper as the class brainstorms.
- Have the students choose a food from the list.
- Ask them each to write a description of that food using as many sense awakening words as possible.

- Explain that the objective is to make their choice of food as realistic an experience as the plate of spaghetti was.

SHARE IT

- Gather the children in a writing circle to read their pieces.
- Encourage classmates to comment on all the ways that they are experiencing that food choice.

CONTINUE IT

- In the reading groups or read-aloud, stop and ask the children if, in their listening or reading, any of their senses has been awakened.
- In their guided reading, have the students copy down words and phrases that they think awaken their senses.
- Copy off a favorite poem, read it aloud and then have one student be the maestro and conduct it. Do this at least twice a week.

NEW HABITS

- On an empty wall area or cupboard door, designate categories of the five senses. Assign students homework for collecting words for these areas, e.g.: words that help us have a virtual smelling experience: *skunk-like; powder-fresh;* OR a tasting experience*: sweet, bitter, lemony.* Continue this pattern with each sense.

Session 2: VISITING THE SEASHORE

Materials needed:
- *Photocopies of* The Seashore Book *text for each student to be used through the next two sessions*
- *Chart with the five senses listed across the top*
- *Pencil and paper for each student*

WHY THIS SESSION

The students will recognize and list examples of five-sense phrases and descriptive words that are found in the mentor text, *The Seashore Book.* This session furthers students' concepts of the power of words to express the five senses.

SAY IT

We found how our senses could definitely be awakened by a use of luscious words to describe food. Now we will read a book about the seashore and notice how the vocabulary awakens our five senses so that we think that we are at the beach.

SHOW IT

Hand out a copy of the text of *The Seashore Book* to each student. The students will turn the text into a personal workbook.

DISCOVER IT

- Instruct the children to raise their hand whenever they hear something in the text that awakens one of their senses as it is read.
- Have them identify which sense is awakened.

NOTE IT

- As each student identifies a sense awakened, note with a mark under that sense category on the chart.
- At the end of the book, figure out which sense was most often addressed in the text.
- Discuss if that is the sense that the students agree has been most awakened by this text.
- Ask them to go to their seats and draw a picture of a sensory image that is most clearly in their mind from the reading.

CONTINUE IT

- In the reading groups or read-aloud, stop and ask the children if in their listening or reading, any of their senses have been awakened.

- In their guided reading, have the students copy down words and phrases that they think awaken their senses.
- Continue to add to the collection of sensory words.
- Continue to copy off a favorite poem, read it aloud and then have one student conduct it. Do this at least twice a week.

Session 3: SENSORY NOTICING

Materials needed:
- *Pencil and paper for each student*

WHY THIS SESSION

Students combine words from the text of *The Seashore Book* with their own. The students will create a list of sense awakening experiences that they have found from the text of *The Seashore Book.* Applicable, useful words expand the students' vocabulary and visualizing expressions.

SAY IT

We are going to make our own sense-awakening list of seashore words and use the text that we have just read through for the first time to help us. We will go over the text of *The Seashore Book* one more time and choose the sense awakening words and phrases that we like the best.

SHOW IT

- Each student has a copy of the text of the book.
- Explain that the point of this rereading is to give the students an opportunity to underline their favorite sense awakening words and phrases.
- Have them only underline the choices that they particularly like.
- Demonstrate this by reading the first page of the text, choosing some words, and underlining them in a copied text that you have made for yourself.

DISCOVER IT

- Send the students off in pairs and together choose and underline their favorite sensorial phrases or describing words.

EXAMPLES

- the sun warms the cool sand
- the beach is golden gray
- the stones are washed smooth
- tiny brown snail shells
- crabs squaggle at our toes

NOTE IT

- Have the student pairs return to the circle and let each pair share one of their examples, explaining which sense is awakened and how.
- Note each example given on chart paper.

CONTINUE IT

- In the reading groups or read-aloud, stop and ask the children if in their listening or reading, any of their senses have been awakened.
- In their guided reading, have the students copy down words and phrases that they think awaken their senses.
- Continue to add to the collection of sensory words taped on the wall.
- As you write down these phrases, ask the children if there are any that could be added to the categories of sensory words that have been collected on the wall or cupboard.
- Copy off a favorite poem, read it aloud and then have one student be the maestro and conduct it.
- Do this at least every other session.

Session 4: WORD POWER

Materials needed:
- *Pencil and paper for each student*
- *Words and phrases gathered from* The Seashore Book *text*
- *Chart of the activity sheet* **A Beach Moment**
- *The activity sheet* **A Beach Moment**
- *Example of Moment from* **SHOW IT**

WHY THIS SESSION

The students will see that they can create their own sense awakening experience with words. They will continue to see how the abstract word can deepen their understanding of the concrete world.

SAY IT

We saw how the author was able to make us feel like we were at the beach by using five-sense awakening phrases and words. Borrowing some of the words from the text, you are going to create a moment at the beach that makes your fellow students feel like they are at the beach, even though they are sitting right here in the classroom.

First, you need to figure out what the moment is that you want to relate to your fellow students. The activity sheet I hand out will help you do that.

SHOW IT

- Distribute the activity sheet **A Beach Moment**
- Demonstrate choosing a moment and note it on the chart, e.g. The moment you want to share is the moment of picking up a beach stone. You want others to feel the beach stone too," so you might write: ***"The sun was warming the cool sand**. I bent down to look at the shiny stones. They glistened in the sun. I picked one up and felt how it had **been washed smooth by the waves."***
- Point out how you used some of the sense words and phrases from the text's list (*in bold print*) to help communicate the idea.

DISCOVER IT

- Place the children with partners to share the moment that they want to write about at the beach.
- Before they pair off, suggest what some of those moments could be: finding a crab; feeling the sun on their shoulders, the water washing over their toes, etc. Encourage them to consider as many moments from the book as possible before picking one to describe.
- Fill in only the top part of the activity sheet.

NOTE IT

- Have the students return to the circle and share all the moments that they plan to write a 2-3 sentence description about.
- List their responses on a chart paper for all to view.
- Children may decide to change their moments and use moments that have been offered.

BRAVE IT

- Direct the students to their work places and have them write the moment by completing the bottom part of the activity sheet.
- Encourage them to use the words from the created list, as well as some of their own rich language.
- When they have finished, have them draw a picture of what they have described. They can make a poem from their words.
- They have read and worked with poems for many sessions now, so you can expect them to be able to write a poem as instructed.

SHARE IT

- The students return to the circle and share as much as they have written.
- Encourage classmates to comment on what senses were particularly awakened with each reading.
- At the end of the sharing, always give students time to voice what was a challenge to them.

CONTINUE IT

- At morning meeting sharing time, have students begin to think of a moment that happened the previous evening on the way to school and say a sentence about it that awakens a sense.
- Continue to add to the collection of sensory words.
- Copy off a favorite poem, read it aloud, and then have one student maestro it. Do this at least twice a week.

NEW HABITS

When you or a student explain something, focus on and encourage using words that awaken the senses.

EXAMPLES:

At the Beach

At the beach
In the summer
The water is shiny and warm
the waves go sky high
then splash and splatter

Annaliese, 3rd grade

Stones and Crabs

Shiny stones
glisten in the sand
as crabs
squaggle round
under the warm sun.

Noah, 2nd grade

Session 5: WHAT THE WORLD IS LIKE

Materials needed:
- *Pencil and paper for each student*
- *Chart paper or smartboard for gathering phrases from the book.*
- Owl Moon, *by Jane Yolen*

WHY THIS SESSION

The students will continue scaffolding their vocabulary by using mentor texts. Owling is not as familiar an experience as going to the beach, but through "awakening the senses" words, the author helps the readers feel that they are having an experience of owling. There are many other moments that can be written about from this text's vocabulary. Through listening to the mentor text, *Owl Moon,* twice, the students will recognize and list examples of five-sense phrases and description words. The list will eventually inspire the creation of their own writing. The expectations of this exercise are similar but more advanced than *The Seashore Book.*

The describing language is primarily simile and metaphor. Children are already aware of metaphors through their play of make-believe. They are mothers as they play with their dolls. They are jaguars as the fly down the field. They are daunting pirates with a patch on their eye and a wooden sword in hand.

SAY IT

We are going to continue to expand our *image-ination* today. We are going to read a story where an author uses wonderfully poetic language. The book is *Owl Moon,* written by Jane Yolen. I will read it through with no hesitation, at first. Then I will read it through very slowly and when you hear a phrase that awakens your sense, raise your hand and I will write it on the class chart here in the front of the room. This is similar to what we did with *The Seashore Book;* this time the whole class is going to help us write our poems.

SHOW IT

- Read the book through once for pure enjoyment. Alert the students to the fact that there are many comparative phrases and they will have an opportunity to comment on them in the second reading.
- Read the book a second time slowing down for the descriptive metaphoric phrases, to impress those images on the imagination.
- Have the students raise their hand if they think they hear a comparative phrase.
- The list of comparative phrases (metaphors and similes) include the following:

> The trees stood still as giant statues
> The train blew loud and long like a sad, sad song
> It was as quiet as a dream
> Dad made a long shadow; mine was short and round
> The trees stood black and pointy against the sky
> We searched the stars as if reading a map
> The moon's face was like a silver mask
> I could feel the cold as if someone's icy hand was palm-down on my back
> My nose was cold and hot at the same time
> The shadows stained the snow
> The snow was whiter than the milk in a cereal bowl
> I listened so hard that my ears hurt
> My eyes got cloudy with the cold
> The heat of the words filled our mouths
> The owl pumped its wings and lifted off the branch like a shadow
> Hope flies on silent wings

DISCOVER IT

- In the second reading, also encourage students to discover other describing phrases not on the list.

NOTE IT

- As in *The Seashore Book,* chart all the describing phrases that are identified by the students. Make them available to all students either with a common class chart or individual lists.

CONTINUE IT

- Continue to add to the collection of sensory words.
- Copy off a favorite poem, read it aloud and then have one student maestro it. Do this at least twice a week.

NEW HABIT

- At morning meeting or transition times begin to play a game of **pair and compare.**
- In this game students try to give a clearer image of something by comparing it to something that is familiar to other students in the room.
- For example if one says, "I forgot to comb my hair. It's a mess." One wonders how much of a mess. If you compare it to a bird's nest, one can get a picture of how much of a mess.
- Or if you say her voice is unpleasant. You may wonder how unpleasant until one makes a comparison to knives slicing through the ears. Then it is very clear how very shrill and sharp the voice is.
- One can actually draw a picture of a bird's nest on top of a head and knives slicing through ears. Emphasize how vivid the idea becomes when it is communicated with a comparison.
- Suggest other potential comparisons and see if the students can complete them.
- Examples:
    Thin as
    Hot as
    Big as
    Slippery as
    Scary as
    Small as

- From now on, be more conscious in using metaphors in everyday lessons and directions, as well as when students are speaking. Ask them to communicate an idea by comparing it to something.

Session 6: WORDS BECOME IMAGES

Materials needed:
- *Piece of drawing paper for each student*
- *Colored pencils and crayons at each desk or sets of tables*
- *Words and phrases gathered from* Owl Moon

WHY THIS SESSION

The students will choose a phrase from the *Owl Moon* communal list that for them inspires the most poignant image. In other words, best incites their five senses *image-ination*. They will draw this image and label it with the describing words from the text. The students are made further aware of how words can draw images.

SAY IT

All these phrases that we have listed from *Owl Moon* have given us very clear pictures in our minds. For example: the "trees are standing still" and are "black and pointy against the sky." We can see the trees standing in a line at attention. They are like soldiers guarding a palace, but they are guarding the forest. You students will draw this image and label it with the describing words from the text or with your own describing words. Example: *They are like soldiers at attention. Or they are black and pointy.* Let's practice: Who can choose one of these phrases on the chart that we read from the book, and tell the class what the image is that comes to your mind when you read the phrase and what you might draw.

SHOW IT

- Scaffold the students' thinking for their own ideas by choosing two or three children to offer suggestions about the phrase that they might choose and the image that they see in their mind.

BRAVE IT

- Give each student a piece of blank paper.
- Place the children in pairs and have them discuss the images that they plan to draw.
- Once they feel confident in what they are going to draw, they may go to a place by themselves and draw their pictures.
- Once they have finished their picture, on a separate piece of lined paper, have them write the phrase that they have chosen to illustrate from the list.
- Ask them to add some of their own describing ideas as well, encouraging them to make comparisons in their efforts to describe.

- Encourage legible writing because their classmates will have to be able to read what they have written.

SHARE IT

- Have the students return to the circle and share their drawing and the text that they have created to describe their drawing.

CONTINUE IT

- Throughout the week, have them continue to work on the drawing of the image.
- Encourage them to include the details of how they see the illustration that they saw in the book.
- The more elaborate their pictures are, the greater potential for a successful poetic writing experience.
- Continue to add to the collection of sensory words.
- Continue using metaphors in everyday lessons and directions as well as when students are speaking, asking them to communicate their idea by comparing it to something.

Session 7: TOGETHER WE WRITE

Materials needed:
- *Drawn images with a piece of paper noting the student's chosen phrase and their additional describing ideas using comparisons*
- *Tape that will stick on the wall*
- *Several pads of 4" x4" sticky notes*
- *Legal-size envelopes for all the students*

WHY THIS SESSION

The students will comment on each of their fellow students' images. Using the sticky notes, they will use descriptive comparative language. Students inspire one another as they work together.

SAY IT

You will notice that I have hung the pictures all around the room. This is the first step in preparing to write your poem inspired from *Owl Moon.* All of you are going to travel around the room with a packet of large sticky notes and think of other comparisons or good describing words that come to mind when you see your classmates' pictures. Please put your initials on your sticky note so the artist can know who has commented on her/his picture. When we all have commented poetically on each picture, the creator of the picture will have lots of phrases to work from to create his/her poem. Use your best handwriting so your classmates can read your beautiful ideas. Remember to use comparisons and rich language when you are commenting on your fellow students' pictures.

SHOW IT

- Stand before one of the pictures and demonstrate.
- Show for example the "shadow-stained snow." Question the students to consider how else it could be said or what else is noticed. A suggestion might be describing it as an *"ink spill on a carpet of white."*
- Then write this down on the sticky note.
- Write your name next to the comment.
- Stick it under that picture.
- Then demonstrate moving on to the next picture.
- This is the procedure the students should follow throughout this session.
- Every student should comment on every picture.
- At the end of the exercise each student should have about 20 new inspired descriptive, comparative phrases from their classmates.

DISCOVER IT

- Have the students gather all the shared ideas about their pictures and place them into an envelope.

NOTE IT

- Have the students spread the comments out on their desks. They can enjoy reading what others have said about their pictures.
- At this time, if they cannot read a comment, they should go to the student named on the sticky note and ask for a "translation."
- Instruct the children to write a list of all the gathered comments that are in the envelope.
- As they do this, they can think about and add new comparative ideas and describing words.
- This list will be used in the next session to create the final poem.

Session 8: A FEAST OF FINE LANGUAGE

Materials needed:
- *Each student's list of descriptive phrases about their pictures*
- *Piece of paper and pencil*
- *Chart of the **Sample List** and three ways to approach a poem (see below in **Show It**)*

WHY THIS SESSION

The students will create their own poems, using their drawn images and gathered poetic language. They will discover that communal writing can be rewarding.

SAY IT:

You now have a buffet of language that you can feast upon to create a delicious poem. You have all this scrumptious language in your gathered list to help you write a description filled with image-producing comparisons. When you finish you can make it into a poem. I am going to take this example of a list written by past students and show you three ways that you could approach your writing.

SHOW IT

Sample list:
- the sky is gray
- scary black shadows
- black as dark ink
- darkness follows scattered trees
- the sky is a smear of dark pudding
- the trees seem ready to attack
- the moon is a hole in the sky

Three Ways to Approach a Poem:
1. Stretch the idea
2. Combine a few
3. Pretend you are there

Stretch the idea: Take one idea communicated in a phrase and then stretch it into something that is bigger than the one noted. For example, take the phrase "the sky is gray" and stretch it to: *The sky is elephant and wrinkly gray.* Then think what else is happening: *Night is sneaking in and the moon is following behind.*

Combine a few: Take a few of the phrases and combine them. It may provide inspiration to add more of one's own or just be happy with writing a combination. The following phrases include the sample list above (the sample list words are in italics):

> Scary *black shadows* are all around
> The night is as *black as dark ink*
> There is only *the moon, a hole in the sky.*

Pretend that you are there: Imagine that you are standing right there in the picture to help stimulate one's senses. For example, begin with:

> *The sky is a smear of pudding, as I trudge through the*
> *heavy snow. Behind me gray footprints follow.*

Students begin to explain the scene as if they are there. They describe this imagined environment with descriptive phrases.

DISCOVER IT

- The students will have an opportunity to try all of these approaches but now they must decide which one they will begin with.
- Place the children in pairs and have them discuss and decide which approach they each will venture first.

NOTE IT

- Have the students gather back in the writing circle and check in with any problems.
- Refer the problems to the class to see if they have ideas for answers to their fellow classmates' questions.

BRAVE IT

- Allow students who wish to work with another student for this first approach, to do so. Some children need that extra confidence.
- At least one of the approaches should be attempted independently as the objective is to get each student language–confident and feel the thrill of individual success.

SHARE IT

- At the end of each effort to create their poems, provide a sharing time where classmates may comment on the images that have been generated by the pieces of writing.

CONTINUE IT

- Students can go back to the text of *Owl Moon* and see if they can find any more ideas for poems. They can venture away from the three designated approaches and just create an individual poem.

- Don't forget to copy off a favorite poem, read it aloud and then have one student maestro it. Do this at least twice a week.
- Continue to allow students who are creating a piece of writing to work in pairs, as their combined ideas can give them confidence for greater creativity.

EXAMPLES:

Winter Trees

The trees are like statues
on a pedestal.
They make gray shadows
on the snow.
They stand in a line
of black pointiness.

Dejohn, 2nd grade

The Moon

The night was dark as an abyss
and then boom the moon appeared
and scared away the darkness.

Micah, 2nd grade

Quiet as a Dream

The trees were quiet as a dream
with no voice
only colors
of a shadow.

Helena, 2nd grade

The Sky

The Sky
makes
a big black hole
that
sucks in
the moonlight.

Trevor, 2nd grade

The Bright Moon

The bright moon fills the dark black sky
The chilly moon fills the cool night air
The gigantic moon is the father of the stars
The chilly moon fills the cool night air.
The moon is like a giant face.
The chilly moon fills the cool night air.

Anika, 2nd grade

The Stars

The stars surrounded the moon
as if it was a prisoner.

Snow was so white and beautiful
I look up into the sky and love it.

The owl howls as if it was a dog.

The moon is as big as a statue
shining on the haunting hoot of the owl.

Sam, 2nd grade

Winter Moon

The bright yellow moon
and white stars
look down
as I trudge through
heavy snow.
Behind me
follow gray footprints.

DeJohn, 2nd grade

Name _____

SPAGHETTI text

The plate arrives at the table. The plate has been warmed in the oven so it is hot to the touch. You wonder how hot so you touch it and jump back, yelling "ow!" and a little red dot appears at the end of your finger where you have burned yourself. You can still hold your fork. You place the cold smooth metal fork between your fingers. You plunge the fork into the steamy pile of noodles covered with the thick tomato sauce. A hot, delicious "tomatoey" smell fills your nose. You begin to wind the noodles round and round your fork until you have a perfect-size ball of noodles wrapped around your fork. You slip this into your mouth and dark red tomato sauce smears the corner of your mouth and drips down your chin. You have not even swallowed the warm clump of tomato and pasta but already your hunger is quieted. "Mmmm, mmmm," you smile and dive your fork in for another bite.

Name _____

A BEACH MOMENT

What is the moment at the beach that you want to share?

_____

_____

_____

How would you describe this moment using your own words and words from the *Seashore Book* text? Remember to use comparisons.

_____

_____

_____

_____

_____

_____

_____

_____

_____

✦ Lesson 4: Beginning Choosing the Right Word

Explicit **Poetic Element Instruction:** Beginning Choosing the Right Word
Implied **Poetic Element Learning**: Image and Comparison; Rhythm; Heart and Message

WHY THIS LESSON

An objective for writers of any genre is to choose the best word for a text. Why does a writer choose the word "rock" over the word "stone"? Is it the heavy sound of the consonants in rock or the crystal-like ping of the letter sounds in stone? Has a stone a reputation of being smaller than a rock? Does it assist the sentence with its rhythmic flow? These kinds of considerations are mulled over in a writer's mind in an instant. That is, their word awareness has been developed.

With word awareness the writer chooses words through sound knowledge and content probing. The writer has played with alliteration, assonance, consonance, repetition, and, of course, rhymes and knows how the sounds of words can slide together rhythmically. The writer has explored the possibility of meaning and knows how a rock can be different from a stone. As a mother coddles and observes her newborn babe, the writer similarly scrutinizes words and imagines their possibilities.

Session 1: LETTER LISTENERS

Materials needed:
- **Hear The Sounds** *activity sheet*
- *Chart paper for categorizing the alphabet into sounds of strong/hard and soft/smooth*
- *Chart paper, for noting the* **Hear The Sounds** *activity sheet results, with two categories of 1) Soft and Hard, and 2) Rhythmic Flow*
- *Pencils for each student*

WHY THIS SESSION

The students will choose what they consider to be the best word for a sentence primarily based on the sound of that word in the sentence. There are no right or wrong answers. The objective of the lesson is to encourage children to be thoughtful about their word choice.

SAY IT

For this session we are going to focus on choosing a word for its sound. Let's begin by sorting the alphabet letters into two categories: 1) strong and hard; and 2) soft and smooth. As you see, I have written them on the chart. As I say a letter, we will do a quick poll and the majority of students will decide in which category we should place the letter. I will begin by putting all the short vowels in the soft, smooth column. I model this because I think when I say /a/ or /i/ it is a soft, soothing sound; while a /p/ or /t/ sounds more harsh and rough. If we can't decide quickly about a letter, we can put it in both columns. (Finish the above sorting exercise. Place the chart of sorted-by-sound letters in an easily visible place in the room, and then continue.)

When writers choose words for their writing, the sounds are important. If the writer is making a very strong statement, then the words chosen will be more effective if they sound strong and hard. If the writer is communicating a soft, quiet idea, then the words chosen will be more effective if they sound soft and soothing.

Another sound consideration of a word is how it fits with the other words in the sentence. When reading, we want the words to flow together with a rhythm and sound that is pleasant and easy to hear, read, and understand.

I am going to give you an activity sheet where you will read a sentence and decide: 1) If the sentence idea needs a word that is strong and hard, or soft and soothing; and 2) You will decide which word gives the sentence a flowing rhythm.

SHOW IT

- Read the directions to the **Hear the Sounds** activity sheet aloud to the class.
- Emphasize that there are many things that a writer has to consider when choosing the right word. Sound is an important factor.
- Model the first sentence for the class.
- Read the sentence with each word choice.
- Ask the students whether they would use "fly" or "zoom" and why.
- Then explain your own choice
- For example, perhaps you chose "fly" because it is a soft word beginning with a soft /f/. Zoom is a hard word, as it begins with a hard /z/ sound.
- Then perhaps you chose *fly* for the sentence because you thought that the fairies are sprinkling magic, which sounds like a soft activity.
- Also you noticed that *fly* and *fairies* begin with the same letter, so the word "fly" makes the sentence rhythmic and pleasant to listen to.
- Ask if there are any students who think that "zoom" may be the best choice.
- Have them explain why.
- Though there is no right or wrong answer, the answer needs to be a thoughtful choice. Ask the students to justify their choices.

DISCOVER IT

- Have the students individually complete their activity sheets.
- As they do the sheets, remind them, while pointing to the chart, to consider choosing a word because of 1) its sound of *soft* or *hard*; AND/OR because of 2) its *rhythmic flow.*
- When they have finished, have them get into pairs and discuss their choices.
- Their discussion will be in preparation for a group discussion in the circle.
- Tell the students to notice how and why they made choices different from their fellow classmates.
- The reasons for different choices are what will be shared when the students return to the writing circle.

NOTE IT

- When finished, bring the students back to the circle.
- Discuss why they have made the choices that they did.
- Note on the chart for each sentence: 1) Why students chose a soft or hard word; 2) Why the word helps the sentence to flow rhythmically.

CONTINUE IT

- In the reading groups, ask the children to find the hard words and soft words on a page.
- Ask them to find words that make a nice rhythm when they are read together.

Session 2: MEAN WHAT YOU SAY

Materials needed:
- **What is Happy** *activity sheet*
- *Pencils for each student*
- *Chart paper with two columns labeled* **WORD** *and* **MEANING**

WHY THIS SESSION

The students will practice choosing words based on the meaning of the idea and sentence they wish to communicate.

SAY IT

For this session we are going to choose words with more of a focus on their meaning than on their sound. We will take a word that could have many meanings depending on what the message is in the sentence. Let's take the word *happy.* One can be really happy, a little bit happy, not so happy, or extremely happy. There are words in our language that can express all those kinds of happiness. A writer must carefully pick just the right "happy" word to communicate the meaning of the sentence. I will give you an activity sheet where you will pick the *happy* word that best communicates what you think is the idea in the sentence.

SHOW IT

- Read the directions to the activity sheet **What Is Happy** aloud to the class as well as all the words that can mean happy. Do not give the definitions of the words. The students will create their own idea of word awareness through discussion with their peers.
- Do the first sentence together.
- Ask for suggestions.
- When the students give a suggestion, ask them why they chose that word.
- What does that word mean to them?
- Have a chart with two columns labeled **WORD** and **MEANING.**
- The word will have different meanings to different people.
- Note all the meanings that the students attribute to each word.
- Let the conversation happen among the students as they discover their own definitions.
- Do not judge or correct the choices of the students.

DISCOVER IT

- Have the students individually complete their activity sheets.
- When they have finished, have them get into pairs and discuss their choices.

- If, in these pair discussions, a student decides to change a word, then of course, that is fine.
- Their discussion will be in preparation for a group discussion in the circle.
- Tell the students to notice how and why they made choices different from their fellow classmates.
- The discussion of why the students have different choices will serve as a learning tool in the students' search for word meaning.

NOTE IT

- When the students have finished their "pair shares" have them return to the circle.
- Continue to add their interpretations to the chart and discuss their reasons for their choices.

CONTINUE IT

- Have the students look at recent writing that they have done and see if they can find words that they can replace with, words that have a clearer meaning for communicating their idea.

NEW HABITS

- When conferencing with a student about writing, focus and comment on using words that best communicate the student's thoughts.

Session 3: SHOW DON'T TELL

Materials needed:
- **Show Me, Don't Tell Me** *activity sheet*
- *Pencil for each student*
- *Chart titled* **SHOWING WORDS**

WHY THIS SESSION

When students are considering words to use in their writing, they must think about sound and meaning as has been practiced in the last two sessions. As well, they must choose words that **SHOW** the reader what they are saying, not just **TELL ABOUT** their message. Students will advance their understanding of choosing words that show, don't just tell.

SAY IT

We can appreciate how difficult it is to choose our words when writing because we have to think about the sound of the words and the meaning. As well, we need to choose words that **show,** not just **tell.** That is, we need to choose words that awaken the five senses. We focused on this in Lesson 3, and now we are going to advance our understanding of that idea.

For example, if we had a sentence in a poem or a piece of writing that said, "the wind blows," we don't get much of an image. We are just told about the wind blowing. But if the text read, "the wind blows through frosty lips turning the trees to silver," then we are really shown this wind. We can imagine what it looks like and feels like. It's cold and harsh and the tree branches are coated with frost and snow. It is your job as writers and poets to use pleasant sounding and meaningful words, as well as awaken the reader's senses. I will hand out an activity sheet that has words that just tell us, they do not show us. Your job will be to awaken the reader's senses.

SHOW IT

- Pass out activity sheet **Show Me, Don't Tell Me**
- The words and phrases on the activity sheet only tell, they do not show.
- It will be the students' responsibility to change the telling into a showing.
- Do the first one together as a class.
- Example; *He went away.*
- Explain that you cannot see "he" nor how he "went," nor where he went "away" to.
- Ask for clarifying suggestions for each area of confusion.
- Students might even suggest that "he" was an animal. *He,* a horse golden as beach sand, *went,* zipped like a strike of lightning, *away,* across the open prairie.

- Remind the students how effective comparisons can be to communicate an important idea.
- Encourage them to use comparisons.
- Repeat this mantra of "show don't tell," over and over throughout all these lessons.

DISCOVER IT

- Have the students work in pairs, then return to the circle to share.

NOTE IT

- As the students share their sentences, chart their "showing" words.
- Particularly note when a student makes a **comparison** to show something.

CONTINUE IT

- In the reading groups or read-aloud, begin to point out to the students where the author or poet has used showing, not telling words.

NEW HABITS

- When the children have finished any written piece, whether it is a story, a reader response, or a nonfiction description, make it now a common practice for students to revise their work by considering whether or not they have chosen words that conjure good, clear images.

Session 4: WISE WORD CHOICE

Materials needed:
- *Chart organized with two columns* **CHOICE** *and* **WHY**
- **Wise Word Choice** *activity sheet*

WHY THIS SESSION

The students will be able to observe that in all genres, writers make careful choices of words, not only because of their sound, but because of their meaning. These examples are from celebrated, published writers and poets.

SAY IT

Students, we have found through the last sessions that choosing the right word to communicate one's idea, is one of the greatest challenges for all writers. If you want your reader to hear and understand what you want to share or communicate, you must make your meaning clear by choosing words for their meaning as well as their sound. We are going to look at some famous writers and see what we can learn from their choices of words.

SHOW IT

- Pass out the **Wise Word Choice** activity sheets.
- Do the first blank of the Langston Hughes poem with the whole class.
- Discuss the difference between *give* and *bring*. Have a student dramatize giving you something and bringing you something. Have them fetch something for you and then talk about the process of creating.
- All these actions involve a different, although subtle process. It is up to the student to decide which process best communicates the message that they want to share.
- After these actions are dramatized, have the students make a choice.
- Again there is no wrong choice.
- You can tell them what the published poet chose, but encourage and respect student choices.

DISCOVER IT

- Put the class into pairs.
- In pairs, they will discuss and choose a word for each blank on the activity sheet.
- Remind them to think about rhythm, meaning, and showing, not telling.
- Have them return to the circle and discuss their choices after completing each example text.
- Share the published writer's choices after the class discussion.
- If their choices are different from the published writer's choices there will be an important learning discussion.
- Do not rush through this exercise. Take time with the discussion.

Regarding the Activity Sheet:

In Exercise 1 Langston Hughes, chose:
1. *Bring*
2. *Bring*
3. *Wrap*

- The two "brings" offer a rhythmic pleasantness. The /ng /makes the words soft and it is a soft message. Bring is not as demanding in meaning as the other choices.
- "Wrap" is a soft word for a soft poem and suggests a careful storing away of the fragile dreams.

In Exercise 2 J.K. Rowling chose:
1. *starts* (Makes rhythm next to the word "story")
2. *sky* (Continues the rhythm of /s/ and directs the reader to where the clouds are specifically)
3. *suggest* (continues the rhythm of /s/ and fewer words and to the point)
4. *mysterious* (continues the rhythm of /s/ and pulls in the reader more quickly than the other words)
5. *soon* (again the continued rhythm of /s/)

In Exercise 3 E.B. White, chose:
1. *slowly*, (gives the clearest image; you can't see the other two words; the /s/ is rhythmic with stairs.)
2. *approached* (in one word says it all)
3. *wobbled* (gives the clearest image. Soft word for a soft moment in the story)
4. *lifted* (rhythmic with the word "lid")
5. *looking up at her* (establishes the connection between Fern and Wilbur from the moment they meet, looking into each other's eyes.)

NOTE IT AND SHARE IT

- When the teacher brings the pairs of students back after each exercise is completed, note on **CHOICE** and **WHY** chart what the teams say about their word choices.
- Ask the teams to justify their choices. Their choices may be more interesting than the author's.
- Continue to ask them if the words that they are choosing bring out the meaning of the sentence and whether or not it assists the rhythm of the poem or prose and does it "show not tell"?
- Also point out that it is not just in poetry that an author tries to find the right word. As shown in the exercises, it is important in all writing.

CONTINUE IT

- In the reading groups or read-aloud, stop and ask the children why certain words in the text have been chosen and whether or not they agree with the published poet's choice.

NEW HABITS

- When the children have finished any written piece, whether it is a story, a reader response, or a nonfiction description, make it common practice for a student to make revisions by considering whether or not chosen words communicate most effectively.

Session 5: SIX WORD MAGNET MAGIC

Materials needed:
- *Magnetic poetry kit (order from Amazon)*
- *Steel cookie sheet*
- *10 steel pie tins (or enough for teams of three students)*
- *Pencil and paper for all students*
- *A chart of the poem* Dark Skies From Leaving *in the* **SHOW IT** *section*
- *A prepared chart with three categories: 1) image; 2) rhythm; 3) words that show don't tell*

WHY THIS SESSION

Students will create poems from six "rich" magnetic words that "show don't tell." This session will deepen the children's appreciation for word choice.

SAY IT

Students, for the past sessions, you learned to notice rich, "showing" language. Now I am going to give you the rich language and you can create wonderful, rich poetry from it. On this cookie sheet are magnetic words that are organized into three categories: Verbs, nouns and describing words, i.e. *adjectives and adverbs. (If the students do not know these basic parts of speech, stop and do a lesson on grammatical parts of speech before going on.)* I will split you up into teams of three and each team will be given a pie plate with the six words. You can work as a team to create a poem or paragraph. You can create them individually. When you finish using these first words, you may come up and choose new words to play with.

SHOW IT

- Choose six magnetic words (two verbs, two nouns, and two describing words) for each pie plate.
- Show the children the words that are magnetized to the pie plate and model how you can push them around to give you ideas.
- The words are supposed to be for ideas, not a complete poem.
- For example: Six words chosen could be: ***nouns:*** sky, cloud; ***verbs:*** leave, remember; ***describing words:*** dark, unknown.
- A model poem using these words is on the chart. Show the prepared chart and point out the use of the magnetized words.

Dark Skies From Leaving

I **remember** the **leaving**
and my mind **darkened**
with the sadness
the days after were **clouded**
with **not knowing**
not caring.
I wondered
if
all my tomorrows
would be filled
with
dark skies
of
hopelessness.

Heidi Simmons

POINT OUT

- You can change the tense or just use the root word.
- You may use words more than once.
- The poem created is filled with many more words than the six given, but the six words serve as a springboard.
- Students do not have to use all the words, if they are satisfied with their creation after using less than six.
- In the model poem, point out the writing strategies most often found in writing. For example, in the poem above, there is an **image** of sadness **compared** to dark weather days.
- There is **rhythm** by a repetition of the /s/ sound in *sadness, days, tomorrows, skies, and hopelessness.*
- **Writing with comparisons shows the idea** rather than **tells it** (The mind is like a dark cloud of not knowing; tomorrow is like a dark sky with no hope.)

BRAVE IT

- Put those who want to work together into groups of three and send them off to separate spaces around the room.
- If a group finishes before others, let them choose their own words and create another poem.

SHARE IT

- Bring the groups of students back after they have completed the exercise.
- Chart three concepts: **images** created by their writing; **rhythm;** and **use of comparisons**.

- Discuss: 1) The images that have been created; 2) The language used to create rhythm; 3) Show don't tell words, particularly comparisons.

CONTINUE IT

- Switch the teams around or encourage students to do it on their own.
- Have a station continually open of "magnetic poetry" which can be played with during free time or when work is completed.
- The poems created can be added to the students' growing poetry collection.

NEW HABITS

- Encourage practice of these three ways of assessing their writing: 1) Do the words give clear images? 2) Is there rhythm in their writing? 3) Are the words that they choose, "showing not telling" language, enhanced with comparisons?

Name _____

Hear the Sounds

FIRST:

Below are words in pairs.
Put an *H* by the words that you think are hard.
Put an *S* by the words that you think are soft.

SECOND:

Fill in the blanks of the sentences with the word that you think is the better choice. Both words mean about the same, but they have different sounds. You might choose a soft word because the idea in the sentence is **soft**, or the idea is **hard** and you choose to use a hard word.

Also, consider how your choice sounds with the other words in the sentence. Choose words that make the sentence pleasantly rhythmic.

1. fly_____
   zoom _____
   Fairies_____ far over the land sprinkling magical dust of happiness.

2. glowed _____
   sparkled_____
   The forest was black with night but in the far distance a campfire _____ in the gloomy night.

3. whispering_____
   mumbling_____
   The court was called to order but still in the back row could be heard the angry _____ of the women.

Name _____

4. punched_____

    hit _____

    He did not want to harm her so he just hardly _____ her.

5. holding_____

    gripping _____

    Greedily_____ the candy bar, he glared at his sister.

6. climbed _____

    scampered _____

    The squirrel _____ up the tree to safety.

7. galloped_____

    ran_____

    The girls _____ across the open field
    throwing their arms open to the glorious sun

8. wound_____

    cut _____

    She carefully wrapped the cloth around the _____ and
    the bleeding stopped.

9. bustling _____

    moving_____

    She is always busy _____ about bringing
    happiness to all.

Name _____

What Is Happy?

How a word SOUNDS is only one reason to choose to use that word.

We also make a decision about a word because it has just the right MEANING for the idea we want to communicate.

Take the feeling happy, there are many choices:

One can be really happy, a little bit happy, not so happy, or extremely happy. Writers must carefully pick just the right word to communicate their meaning of the sentence.

Below is a list of words that all mean happy, but all mean a different kind of happy. Choose the word that you think best suits the idea communicated in the sentences below.

- glad
- cheerful
- joy
- merry
- proud
- jolly
- delighted
- satisfied
- lucky
- festive

Name _____

1. As Gina cuddled the puppy and buried her face in its fur, she felt so_____.

2. Santa Claus sat in the large velvet seat and laughed a _____ chuckle that made everyone smile.

3. I could not believe that I saw my 3rd grade friend after 10 years. Certainly I was filled with _____.

4. "What? I won the lottery ticket. Man! I am so _____."

5. I braided my hair and wore a colorful skirt. There were firecrackers, loud voices and musical instruments in the air. "Oh my," I exclaimed, "This is such a _____evening."

6. I had not seen my friend for 20 years. I was sooooo _____ to see her once again.

7. It is a special holiday, so grab your neighbor and hug them for it is certainly a time to be _____.

8. I have eaten the dinner and the dessert. I can promise you, I am no longer hungry. I am totally _____.

9. I must tell you, I do not feel very _____tonight because I have a terrible cold.

10. "Today I ran the mile at school for the first time!!! YOW! I am so _____!"

Name _____

Show Me, Don't Tell Me

Below are sentences that do not awaken the senses. Change these **tell me** sentences, into **show me sentences.** Awaken the reader's senses.

1. He went away._____

   _____

   _____

2. She ate the food._____

   _____

   _____

3. They looked at it._____

   _____

   _____

4. He moved it._____

   _____

   _____

5. She got some._____

   _____

   _____

6. She was mad._____

   _____

   _____

Name _____

Wise Word Choice

The Dream Keeper

By Langston Hughes

1. _____me all your dreams
You dreamers

2. _____ me all of your
Heart melodies

That I may 3. _____ them
In a blue cloud-cloth
Away from the too-rough fingers
Of the world.

CHOICES:
1. Give, Bring, Create, Fetch
2. Bring, Pluck, Gather, Carry to
3. Put, Wrap, Hide, Place

Name _____

Wise Word Choice

Harry Potter and the Sorcerer's Stone

By J.K. Rowling

When Mr. and Mrs. Dursley woke up on the dull grey Tuesday our

story 1. _____, there was nothing about the cloudy

2. _____ outside to 3. _____ that strange and

4. _____ things would 5. _____ be happening

all over the country.

CHOICES

1. happens, starts, begins
2. day, morning, sky
3. make you think, suggest, give a clue
4. peculiar, complicated, mysterious
5. now, perhaps, soon

Name _____

Wise Word Choice

Charlotte's Web

By E.B. White

Fern came 1. _____ down the stairs. Her eyes were red

from crying. As she 2._____

her chair, the carton 3._____

and there was a scratching noise. Fern looked at her father. Then she

4._____ the lid. There, inside, 5. _____

was the newborn pig.

CHOICES
1. not happily, slowly, angrily
2. went over to, approached, came to
3. moved, shook, wobbled
4. raised, lifted, opened up
5. sleeping, making grunting noises, looking up at her.

✦ Lesson 5: Choosing the Right Word: Using a Thesaurus and Beginning Personification

Explicit **Poetic Element Instruction:** Advanced Choosing the Right Word
Implied **Poetic Element Learning**: Image and Comparison; Rhythm; Heart and Message

WHY THIS LESSON

At this point, the students have been introduced to the importance of expressing their ideas with words that are visually inspiring, heartfelt, pleasurable in sound, and poignant in thought. A critical component to this goal is choosing the right words. Writers often find help with their word choices from outside resources. In the previous lessons, it is apparent how a mentor text can inspire the word muse. Using a **thesaurus** is equally effective and supports greater independence in word choice. This lesson seeks to give young writers the know-how to become proficient users of a thesaurus in addition to understanding its merit and importance in writing and communicating.

This lesson assumes two prerequisites:

- A previous understanding of basic dictionary skills: Students must have an understanding of how and why one uses a dictionary before they venture into thesaurus use.
- The teacher has a working facility with the thesaurus.

Session 1: THROUGH THE THESAURUS

Materials needed:

- *A comprehensive thesaurus suitable for third, fourth, and fifth graders and beyond is* Roget's International Thesaurus, *by Barbara Kipfer, Ph.D. You will need several "book walk sessions," but the more facile students become with using a thesaurus, the more rewarding it will be. The thesaurus is an important addition to the classroom. If the budget allows, purchase one for every two students.*
- *Pencils for each student*
- *Paper for each student*
- **Using the Thesaurus** *Activity Sheet*

WHY THIS SESSION

The students will learn how to use *Roget's International Thesaurus*. They will learn some of the ways a thesaurus is an important writing tool.

SAY IT

Students, you have learned through our last lessons how challenging and important it is to choose the right word. But sometimes we cannot always think of or know the exact word we're looking for. You have seen how to use words from other texts as we did with Jane Yolen's, *Owl Moon*. Now you will become more independent and learn to figure out your own right words by using a thesaurus.

A thesaurus is alphabetized like a dictionary but instead of using definitions to explain the meaning of a word, it lists words with similar meanings, allowing an increased understanding of similar words so we can say what we mean more exactly. Several words with similar meanings not only help us understand what one particular word means, but also help to make a text more interesting by allowing for a greater variety of vocabulary in a text. Let's look at this thesaurus to understand what I am talking about.

SHOW IT

- Introduce the students to the basic skill of using this thesaurus. They must figure out the word they want, alphabetically listed in the back. And then go to the designated number, enumerated in the front.
- Do not hand out the activity sheets until all students are comfortable using this resource.
- Hand out the activity sheet, **Using The Thesaurus.**
- Do the first activity together with the students.
- Move slowly; *Roget's International Thesaurus* can be daunting at first, but with practice becomes a very good friend.
- Have the students work in pairs.

DISCOVER IT

- In pairs, have the students do the rest of the activity sheet.
- Stop after each activity to discuss the challenges and rewards of using this vocabulary tool.

NOTE IT

- The introduction to the thesaurus and the activity sheet will take several sessions. Keep an ongoing chart of class comments about the experience.

CONTINUE IT

- Ask the students to follow this procedure with other commonly overused words like: *went, said,* and *eat.*

NEW HABITS

- Have the thesauruses conveniently available in the classroom, so they may be used during all writing efforts.
- During writing revision, encourage students to use the thesaurus to get ideas for more exact and interesting words in their writing. Make using a thesaurus a habit.

Session 2: REALIZING THE RANGE OF OUR FEELINGS

Materials needed:

- *A chart of six major feelings: Anger, Surprise, Joy, Fear, Sadness, Love*
- *Pencil and paper for each student*
- *Available thesauruses*
- *The activity sheet that they completed on* **What is Happy** *in Lesson 4. If they do not have it, they can do it before continuing with this session.*
- *Vertically lined (if available) card stock strips (approx. 3"x24"); horizontal sentence strips can be used if necessary*

WHY THIS SESSION

The students have explored the use of "happy" in the previous lesson. This session gives the students an opportunity to explore, through the thesaurus, a range of emotions as well as the many choices available for words to communicate those emotions.

SAY IT

Students, think back to when we talked about all the ways to express the word, "happy." If you just won a free trip to Disney World, how would you express your happiness in words? A few sessions ago, you might have said "I am very, very, very, very happy!" Now that a thesaurus has introduced you to some other words, you might say, "My smile reaches around my face, I am ecstatic!" Certainly, the second example communicates your feelings more clearly than the first. "Ecstatic" expresses an extremely happy feeling. "Content" expresses a different kind of happy. Who can share a time when you felt content?

Emotions cannot be measured at one particular degree. They are not all just about 55 degrees. Sometimes I can be mad at 212 degrees and that is when I am at my boiling point. I am furious. And sometimes I am mad at 90 degrees when I am feeling annoyed and cranky. We are going to explore words that can express the full range of six major feelings.

You have already worked with a list of happy words. Let's start with this list by arranging the words from the most happy to the least happy.

[*Have the children do this in pairs and then share their results. There is no absolute right order but ask them to explain why they have chosen to place a word as less or more happy on the list.*]

This was a rehearsal for what you will do with your choice of one of these six emotions that I have listed on the chart. Use a thesaurus to research at least ten to fifteen synonyms of your emotion of choice. Once you have made a list of ten to fifteen words, arrange them from the lesser example of this emotion to the most extreme. We will make final lists on paper strips and hang them around the room. You and your classmates will be able to reference them in your writing.

SHOW IT

- Practice the procedure by taking the word "*sad*" and looking it up in the thesauras. There are already several synonyms in the thesauras and those can be copied.
- From this "paragraph of words" one can choose more words to complete a range of feelings.
- The list is completed when the student has accumulated ten to fifteen words with which they are familiar.

DISCOVER IT

- The students have been placed in pairs and have a list of chosen words.
- In their pairs, the students will discuss the justification for their ordering of the words they have chosen.
- If they have found a word in their researching that they may have heard but don't really know, have them look it up in the dictionary.
- Once they have agreed on the order, have the students print the words neatly on a vertical hanging strip.

SHARE IT

- The students will read their lists in the writing circle, and share a new or favorite word with their classmates.
- Encourage questions, comments, or discussion on the order of the words.

CONTINUE IT

- Use magazines to find images of an animal or human expressing the chosen emotion that can be glued on their list, giving the emotion a visual indicator.

NEW HABITS

- Encourage the students to practice naming emotions more specifically when they are speaking or writing.

Session 3: FEELINGS COME ALIVE

Materials needed:
- **Personify Your Emotions** *activity sheet*
- *Pencil and paper for each student*
- *Gendler, Ruth (1988).* The Book of Qualities, *NY, NY: Harper Collins*

WHY THIS SESSION

Young students can understand an abstract idea like an emotion when it is given a concrete comparison by using a simile, metaphor, or personification. This session will give them practice at expressing emotions using personification. At the same time, they will deepen their dictionary and thesaurus skills.

SAY IT

Students, what if all the emotions that are represented on your *range of emotions lists*, suddenly came alive? What do you think "grouchy" would act like? What would "exuberant" be wearing? Who would "hopeless" want to hang out with? What would they do for entertainment?

I will hand out the **Personify Your Emotions** activity sheet with some examples from students your age to help inspire *you* to bring emotions to life.

SHOW IT

- Read aloud the models from the activity sheet.
- Look through the Gendler book to find additional personified emotions appropriate for your class.
- Read over the **Think Sheet** (part of the **Personify Your Emotions** activity sheet) and ask what other category one might want to personify an emotion effectively.
- Have the students add any new suggestions to their think sheets.

BRAVE IT

- The students can now create their characters.
- Encourage students to continue to use the thesaurus for adjectives that will help describe their emotion.

- Emphasize using vivid describing words and comparisons to describe the emotion clearly and exactly.

SHARE IT

- The students will share their personifying paragraphs in the writing circle.
- Encourage the class to discuss the visual experience each student's piece of writing inspires.

CONTINUE IT

- After the discussion, the students can draw their emotion or make a collage from illustrations in a magazine.
- Students can create more than one personification of an emotion. The more they do, the deeper the understanding of the emotion becomes.

NEW HABITS

- Continue to encourage the students to name emotions as specifically as possible in their speaking and writing.

PEER EXAMPLES *(included on the activity sheet)*

FRUSTRATION

Frustration can never get something done correctly. He tries again and again, but it never comes out right.

Frustration has a wrinkled nose because he is very angry. Worry comes over for tea, but he always spills his. Frustration has a black coat, but the buttonholes are too small, so it is always unbuttoned.

Frustration carries a briefcase which always falls open and papers fly everywhere.

Addison, 4th grade

SHY

Shy.... we don't really know much about her. She always curls up in a corner. She has never come out. But if you go to her door and knock and look through the window, you see her shiver then dash to the corner.

Shy.....we don't think she can speak and if she could no one knows what her voice would sound like. They assume it is soft and delicate like what she looks like.

Shy sometimes thinks about going out into the world, but when her hand gets close to the door handle, she nearly passes out. Her face turns blank white and again she dashes to her corner.

Teagan, 4th grade

Session 4: WORDS' EVERY ANGLE

Materials needed:
- *Activity sheet* **Exploring The Word From Every Angle**
- *Pencil and paper*

WHY THIS SESSION

It is important to experience words as independent entities, outside of syntax, definition or purpose. Serious writers need to get in touch with the possibility of words, beyond their dictionary meanings. A writer's job is to help the population see the world in unique perspectives and propose ponderous connections. Their tools are words and they must be able to wield them deftly. Therefore, they must understand words from every angle. The art of "word angling" is a basic writing competency.

SAY IT

Students, as writers we know that our most important tool is the word. We have to be as competent in manipulating words as a carpenter is in handling a hammer. A carpenter does not just pick up a hammer and begin banging. He must hold it, grip it, tap it, swing it, feel its weight and respect its power. That is what writers must do with their tool, the word. It is a very powerful tool, but to understand its importance and respect its capability, writers must get to know every angle of it. It is not enough to just look up the definition in the dictionary. That is someone else telling you what the word is. Writers need to figure out what the word means to them and what they can do with it, just as a carpenter needs to figure out what can be done with a hammer.

We are going to start with a very simple word, "table." Perhaps you think there's nothing new to learn about such a common word, but I am going to show you how to explore it from every angle, so that maybe you will soon have a whole new respect for the possibilities and power of the everyday word "table."

SHOW IT

- Hand out the activity sheets **Exploring The Word From Every Angle.**
- Read to the class and explore the first angle of the word, which is that of rhyme and playfulness of the word.
- When you have finished the two lines, ask if anyone can add some more rhyming playful words.
- Read to the class and explore the second angle, what it might be like to be a table. Ask the class if they were a table, what that table would look like and be used for.

- Read the third exploration and discuss what our world would be like if we did not have the word "table." End by asking where they would find it inconvenient or difficult to be without a table.
- They have explored the many angles of the word "table" as a class, now they are going to do the same thing independently or in pairs.
- Complete the activity sheet **Exploring The Word From Every Angle**.

BRAVE IT

- The students, having seen the modeling of the word table, will now choose their own common word. For example: *sink, tree, bed, ladder, tooth brush.*
- Brainstorm and chart a list of common everyday nouns for ideas.

SHARE IT/NOTE IT

- Share student creations in the writing circle.
- After each pair or child has shared, ask both the writers and the listeners what new angle they have discovered with the word that was explored.
- Record the findings.

CONTINUE IT

- Students can create more word angle discoveries, using the ideas from the list brainstormed at the beginning of **BRAVE IT**. The more they do, the more fun and natural "word angling" will become.
- Create a poem from word angling discoveries.

NEW HABITS

- Stop while reading aloud or while in guided reading and consider the curiosity, derivation, perfection, fun-sounding aspects of words.

Name _____

Using the Thesaurus

A thesaurus can be useful in a variety of ways:

1. It can help **clarify and understand one's thoughts**. When we name our thoughts, it is easier to understand them.

   Example:

   You are at home and it is pouring rain. No one else is home and you find yourself feeling very sad. You decide to write about it, but when you sit down, you don't know what the sad really is. You begin the search.

   - Look up the word "sad" in the back of the thesaurus.
   - Pick the word that seems closest to how you feel.
   - Find that word in the numbered part of the thesaurus.
   - Opposite words are also on that page.
   - How does knowing the opposite help get a deeper understanding of a word?
   - Write a first line of a poem of sadness.

2. Use the thesaurus to **find the right sounding word.**

   Example:

   You are writing a poem. The first line is *Minutes tick by fast.* It doesn't **sound right** to you. There is something wrong with the rhythm. Is there another word for fast that would give the rhythm that you are seeking?

   - Look up the word *fast* and see if there is another word that would give you the rhythm that you are seeking.

Name _____

3. Learn **new meanings** for words that you thought only had one meaning.

   Example:
   - Think of the word "gate." What image comes to mind? Look this up and see all the meanings.
   - Pick one of the "gate" words that you are not familiar with.
   - Look it up to see if you can then understand its meaning.
   - Raise your hand when you think you know its meaning.

4. Find the word that **exactly** expresses what you are trying to say.

   Example:
   I want to explain that the waves are really **gentle.** Look up gentle and decide what word best describes a wave to you.
   Write that word below:

   _____

5. It helps discover **all the ways that one word is used** in the English **language.**

   Example:
   - Look up the word "get."
   - Identify a "get" word that you do not know and explain what it means on the line below.
   - On the second and third lines write a sentence using the get word that you have discovered.

   _____

   _____

   _____

Name _____

Practice:

- Below are attempts at poetic phrases.
- Each sentence is a good beginning effort, but clearer images could be created by using the thesaurus.
- Use the thesaurus to explore possibilities for the words in bold type.

*The sun **lay** on the still water.* _____

_____

_____

*The trees swayed in the **nice** breeze.* _____

_____

_____

*The **good** mother gave a big hug to the **unhappy** child.* _____

_____

_____

*The child **ran** after his sister.* _____

_____

_____

*The sun **shines on** the desert all day long.* _____

_____

_____

*My mom **likes** vegetables, but she **loves** chocolate.* _____

_____

_____

Name _____

Personify Your Emotions

Below are examples of emotions that have been personified.

- Read the models below.
- Choose an emotion from your *range of emotions* list from the last lesson.
- Use the **think sheet** on the next page to help come up with ideas about your emotion.
- Write a paragraph personifying your chosen emotion.

WORRY

Worry writes about nervous habits
She makes lines on people's foreheads
Lists everything that's wrong.
She is sure that she left the stove on.
She is most scared about what she doesn't know.

LONELINESS

Loneliness likes to run. He can do it by himself.
He wears his black jacket thrown back across his shoulders. People don't come near. He does not trust being with people. He does not go near joy. He hates happiness.

FRUSTRATION

Frustration has a wrinkled nose because he is very angry. Worry comes over for tea, but he always spills his. Frustration has a black coat, but the buttonholes are too small, so it is always unbuttoned.
Frustration carries a briefcase which always falls open and papers fly everywhere.

Addison, 4th grade

SHY

Shy.... we don't really know much about her. She always curls up in a corner. She has never come out. But if you go to her door and knock and look through the window, you see her shiver then dash to the corner.

Shy.... we don't think she can speak and if she could no one knows what her voice would sound like. They assume it is soft and delicate like what she looks like.

Shy sometimes thinks about going out into the world, but when her hand gets close to the door handle, she nearly passes out. Her face turns paper white and again she dashes to her corner.

Teagan, 4th grade

Name _____

The Think Sheet

Your chosen emotion _____

What does it wear?_____

_____

_____

Is it male, female or neither? _____

_____

_____

What does it like to do?_____

_____

_____

What is it afraid of?_____

_____

_____

Who are its best friends and its enemies? _____

_____

_____

Name _____

Exploring The Word from Every Angle

It is important to experience words as independent entities, outside of grammar, definition or purpose. Writers need to get in touch with the possibility of words; beyond the meanings they were first instructed. A poet's job is to help the population see the world in unique perspectives and propose ponderous connections. Their tools are words and they must be able to wield them deftly. Therefore they must understand words from every angle.

Example: Take the very common word "table." EVERYONE knows what a table is and its purpose, OR maybe you don't.

Explore table with rhyme and playfulness:

Table, bable, an able table upon which I will put a stable of food, a nibble, a dribble is what you might label the food on the table if you are capable.

Explore being a table:

Again, the popsicle has been left upon my head to dribble down my leg and leave a sticky puddle of goo on my foot. The cold circle of wet from the glass of milk has been left and transformed into a white ring scarring my smooth brown surface. Books are clunked down on me heedlessly, I groan but it is lost in the varnish. It is only when company comes that I am pampered and caressed with a soft rag and the perfume of fine oil. A square of clean white cloth is snapped spritely over my head, and wafts quietly down, laid flat and smoothed with ceremony, covering up my bruises and abuses of the previous days.

Name _____

Explore the world without a table:

I am home. I try to throw my car keys on the front hall table. But it does not exist. Clatter, clatter onto the floor they tumble. They are picked up by the dog, and the next day I cannot find the keys and am late to work.

It is time for dinner. I get the plates out but there is no place to put them so I pile them up and place them back in the cupboard. When the food is ready, everyone is given a spoon and we dig into a large common pot.

A desk is a kind of table and at school when we do our work, we now have to kneel on the hard floor, to write. There are cracks in the separated tiles, so our writing jaggles along over the paper and is difficult to read.

What else might happen without a table?

_____

_____

_____

Choose a very common object that everyone knows. People who do not know English can quickly grasp the meaning of this word.

Your Word _____
(Use a separate piece of paper if there are not enough lines for you to finish your work)

Explore the word with rhyme and playfulness: _____

_____

_____

Explore being the word: _____

_____

_____

Explore the world without your word: _____

_____

_____

✦ Lesson 6: Image and Comparison Using Personification

Explicit **Poetic Element Instruction:** Image and Comparison using Personification
Implied **Poetic Element Learning:** Choosing the Right Word; Rhythm; Heart and Message

WHY THIS LESSON

When children maintain that they did not break the glass, rather it broke itself as it hit the floor, they imply a natural inclination to personify the world. The glass was capable of breaking itself! Personification is not only natural to a child but a preferred way of thinking. Children delight in the explanation of their shadow being a dependable buddy who grabs the bottom of their heel and follows them loyally around the yard. Friends and buddies are a familiar concept to a small child. If a child connects the word, *shadow*, to friend, the concept of a shadow becomes familiar and gains personal meaning. Personification helps a child to create personal significance to their vocabulary while nurturing imagination and creativity.

Instructing personification is an effective strategy in assisting children to gain control of and give meaning to their vocabulary.

Session 1: THE ROOM IS ALIVE — PERSONIFICATION

Materials needed:
- *Paper and pencil for each child*

WHY THIS SESSION

The students will use their imaginations to give human characteristics to inanimate objects in their immediate surroundings. The comparisons will help the students to conceptualize the world in new ways.

SAY IT

Students you have made things that are not alive, come alive in our previous lessons. Your emotions wore clothes, had certain friends, even liked particular activities. And the trees and snow and moon came alive when we read *Owl Moon*.

It helped us to visualize and connect with those things. The moon became our buddy. We knew the emotion happiness. It seemed to live next door. When we make things that we can't touch or aren't human come alive, we can connect with them, because they seem more like us. Let's look around the room. Does anyone see the light overhead *staring* at us with her big yellow eye? And how hungry is that pencil sharpener when the pencil gets close to its mouth? Did the happiness you felt when you understood a math problem grab you around the neck and give you a big hug? Did that chair stick out its leg today and trip you?

Now it is your turn to bring this room alive, that otherwise seems sort of asleep. When we do this there is a literary term that we will continue to use more and more. It is personification. We are personifying these objects because we are making something that is NOT a person seem like a person. You may choose a partner or work on your own. You will need to bring alive the *feelings* that happen in this room or the *objects* that presently exist. Choose at least four ideas to write down and we will share them in our writing circle.

SHOW IT

- Go to the chart paper or the smartboard and propose two or three ideas of personification noticed in the room.
- Personify *feelings* like *sadness draped around my shoulders and hung heavily on my neck,* as well as modeling personification of *objects.*
- Modeling gives children a structure within which to work.

DISCOVER IT

- Allow the students to work alone or with partners. Encourage them to walk the room in silence except to whisper to their partners. When they get an idea, they should stop and record it on their papers.

NOTE IT

- When the students have finished, have them come to the circle and share their ideas.
- Share and record each idea. These will be titles or inspiration for writings later on.

BRAVE IT

- Ask the students to choose one of the ideas from their lists to extend into a paragraph.
- If the idea is a pencil sharpener eating a pencil, suggest they talk about the silver belly that the pencil shavings fall into and its sharp grinding teeth.
- The students can begin with a paragraph and then put in line breaks to make it a poem.

SHARE IT

- Have the students share their extended personification paragraph or poem.
- Ask fellow students to respond with the visualizations inspired from the readings.

CONTINUE IT

- Ask the children to draw pictures from the paragraphs or poems they have created.
- In the reading groups or read-aloud, stop and ask the children if they notice a personification in the reading. And whether they think the sentence would be as interesting if the personification were not there.

NEW HABITS

- Place personifying comments on the objects in your classroom. (Examples: Watch out this sharpener eats any pencil; this light is watching you; be careful, the floor has a back pain this morning, etc.)

EXAMPLES OF POEMS FROM THIS EXERCISE

The book hibernates
in my back pack.
Soon its resting season
 will be over.
Soon it will need to feed
a young mind.
Soon my mind will be filled
with its knowledge.

Ava, 4th grade

The pencil sharpener is
very hungry.
Here comes the dinner!
Slowly he slips
wood and lead
into his mouth.
He grumbles as he eats.
Soon he has eaten
most of the pencil.
He is done with his dinner.
Where is dessert?

Frayha, 4th grade

The eraser
it wipes
it cleans
it washes away
the lead from
the paper
then finally
it smiles
at its handy work

Elias, 4th grade

Session 2: AN EPISTLE OF EMPATHY

Materials needed:
- *Paper and pencil for each child*
- *Chart of possible ideas for writing a letter (suggestions on activity sheet)*
- **My Letter To:** *activity sheet*

WHY THIS SESSION

The students will communicate with something very familiar to them and gain a better understanding of it because they connect to it through feelings that they know and understand. This helps the students to gain control of the world on their terms. Some students who struggled with the previous session can do this personification exercise more successfully. Eventually this will help students create metaphors. For example, a student might try to explain a caring fellow student and to get the idea across compare his compassionate friend to a soft pillow always willing to absorb one's tears and not hold judgment. The student will find ideas of metaphoric comparisons from these exercises of personification.

Understanding the attributes of something is a first step in figuring out a metaphor. The student becomes aware of all the possibilities for comparison. Personification supplies infinite possibilities for visualization and expansion of imagination.

SAY IT

In the last session, you made the room come alive. You opened the imagination and found new and inspiring ways to describe and visualize the world around us. Another way to personify something is by writing a personal letter to it. Imagine that it is alive and that you have a close relationship to it. What does it mean to you? Why is it useful? What can you do with it? What does it do for you?

Look at the activity sheet *My Letter To:.* You will see a list of ideas of things you might write to. Think of it as a letter of appreciation or thank you note. You are writing to tell this thing why it is important to you. Let's add to this list of things we'd like to write to. Who can suggest other things to write a letter to? (*List these ideas under the ideas that are already on the chart.*) On the activity sheet, there is an example of a letter written to a pillow.

SHOW IT

- Read the letter aloud.
- Ask the class to suggest other things that could be said to the pillow.

DISCOVER IT

- Have the children write a letter to *their* pillows. They can use ideas from the class discussion.
- Allow the children to work alone or with partners.
- Ask them to jot down how they appreciate a pillow.

NOTE IT

- When the students have finished, have them share their ideas.
- Give the rest of the class an opportunity to respond to the sharer.
- Discuss the students' visualizations and how they affect others' feelings for a pillow.

BRAVE IT

- Now that the students have a good idea of what the expectation of the letter is, have them write their own letters, using an idea of their own or one from the brainstormed list.

SHARE IT

- Before the students read their letters, do not let them disclose the object of their letters. Have the class guess what it is.
- Each guess must be accompanied with an explanation for that guess.

CONTINUE IT

- This is a good exercise for practicing spelling words or Social Studies and Science concepts. They can become the recipient of a personifying letter, e.g. *Dear Segregation:* or *Dear Evaporation:*

NEW HABITS

- When introducing difficult abstract concepts, ask the students what they might say or ask that concept in a letter. The concept may not seem so intimidating, once it feels like someone with whom they can communicate.

Session 3: ACTING OUT

Materials needed:
- **FOG**, *by Carl Sandberg*
- *A youtube example of fog moving along the ground*
- **Personified Poems Acting** *activity sheet*

WHY THIS SESSION

In this session and the next, students will deepen their understanding and extend their practice of personification. No longer are they going to write about what they imagine that an inanimate thing, feeling or concept might be like if it were personified, they are going to BECOME that thing, feeling or concept. They are going to feel it from the inside out. They are going to assume a first-person viewpoint. (*You could certainly use this activity to explain first-person and third-person viewpoint in writing.*) The students will become actors. Students may find it easier to communicate their feelings for the inanimate through enactment. And then once enacting it, with a deeper understanding, they can find the words to write it.

SAY IT

Students, we have been writing about how we think things might be if they were people. At times we might think that we are alone, but now that we have brought our world alive, we now realize our room is very crowded with personalities. Now we are going to jump from being an outsider, imagining what it might be, to actually becoming it by acting it out. We will not use words. We will use only gestures and movement. We will have no props. We must be creative in our movements so our audience knows what we are communicating. There is no one way to interpret a poem through acting. Just as when we read a story or a poem, everyone understands it differently because of our different experiences. We will begin with a famous poem by Carl Sandberg, titled *Fog*. I will first show you a youtube video of fog moving so you can see where Carl Sandberg may have gotten his idea. I will also need someone who really likes to act to volunteer to do some acting in front of the whole class. Everyone will have an opportunity to try it out.

SHOW IT

- Show the youtube video and talk about some adjectives that you might use to describe the moving fog.
- Those vocabulary words could be used when discussing what the students observe in the enactment of the fog.
- Pass out copies of *Fog* and then read the poem and discuss all vocabulary that the students do not understand. (most likely just "haunches")
- Read it out loud very slowly as you watch the fog roll in.

DISCOVER IT

- Ask the student who has volunteered to enact this to listen carefully to the words and then try to become the fog and move like the fog that Carl Sandberg explained while you read the poem aloud again.

NOTE IT

- Once the student volunteer has acted out *Fog*, discuss in what ways the actor acted like the language of the poem seemed to direct.
- These ideas will be useful because the other students are also going to act out the poem.
- They can think about how another student has done it, but encourage them to try different interpretations.

BRAVE IT

- Now that the students have a good idea of what an enactment can look like, pair up the students.
- They do not have to enact it in front of the class unless they wish to, but all need to try out enacting.
- Send the student pairs to separate areas of the room, where one can read the poem while the other enacts it. Then they will change so both have the opportunity for acting.

SHARE IT

- When the students have completed acting with each other, ask if any couple would like to perform in front of the class.
- Compare and discuss the different interpretations.
- Use some of the words that the students proposed from the youtube discussion.

CONTINUE IT

- This enactment of personification will be continued in the next session and after that, personification and metaphors should be enacted often.

NEW HABITS

- Find other opportunities for students to act out abstract ideas. Acting can help children to segue into writing.

Session 4: BECOMING AN OBJECT

Materials needed:
- **Personified Objects Poems** *activity sheet*
- **Personified Poems Acting** *activity sheet*
- *Prepared chart with three categories: 1) object's character, 2) object's human-like actions, 3) connections to object*
- *This session is enriched by using Valerie Worth's book listed in the bibliography*

WHY THIS SESSION

Students will continue to practice becoming the object in their poems. This interaction will prepare them for writing their own personifying poem of an object. They will answer questions on their **Personified Poems Acting** activity sheet that will help them to consider their acting and their own poem creations.

SAY IT

Students, we are going to continue acting out poems and becoming the object that the poem is about. I am passing out a packet of poems that we will use during this session. The poems personify a variety of things and make them seem alive, just like Sandberg personified fog and made it seem alive. We will read each poem, discuss any difficult vocabulary, and maestro them. Then in pairs, using an activity sheet you will further analyze them in preparation for performing them for the class. The performance will be quiet mime, like we did with *Fog*.

SHOW IT

- Hand out the **Personified Objects Poems** activity sheet
- Take one or two sessions to just read, study the vocabulary and maestro the poems.
- Once the poems have been read and vocabulary understood, explain that they will be placed in teams of 3 or 4 and analyze the poem that they have been assigned by filling out an activity sheet.
- Use "The Sun" to begin to model the expectaion of the activity sheet
- Pointing to the prepared class chart, ask the students to suggest one word that could describe the sun's **CHARACTER**. A suggestion could be *crafty.*
- Note the suggestion on the chart.
- Have the students note a word in the poem that suggests the sun's **HUMAN-LIKE ACTIONS**. *Serene* could be suggested and noted on the chart.
- Finally, ask if anyone knows someone like this sun and have a CONNECTION. Perhaps they know someone who has a sweet smile but is mean inside.

- Explain that filling out this activity sheet before enacting the poem, helps the acting team to know and understand how the object has been personified.

DISCOVER IT

- Hand out the **Personified Poems Acting** activity sheets.
- Divide students up into teams of 3 or 4, and assign one of the poems to each team.
- Explain that each team will enact the poem in front of the class.
- Have the children first read it all together and then fill out their activity sheets as was previously modeled with the poem, "The Sun."
- After analyzing the poem in this fashion, they should be ready to practice enacting it.
- One student should read the poem while the others enact it.

NOTE IT

- After each performance, ask the fellow students how the object came alive.
- Ask the performing team how they connected with it.
- By enacting an object the students will have another perspective from which to approach the writing of their own object poems.
- Some students may find that enactment helps to organize their thoughts for writing.

BRAVE IT

- Students are ready to brave their own poem that will personify an object.
- They can choose anything from an object in their room, to something outside the room like a tool shed, kitchen, a plant in the park or their garden, a moon.
- Their poem will be more successful if they know the object well.
- **NO stuffed animals or dolls or puppets. They already have the attributes of a person so the student is not really using imagination. And no pets as they are alive.**
- Brainstorm a list of ideas on the board so the students have an idea of what they can write about.

SHARE IT

- When the students have completed their poems, have them read them aloud.
- After each poem, discuss with their fellow students when the object seems to have feelings or moves and acts like a person.

CONTINUE IT

- Ask which students would like to have their poems enacted as they did with Valerie Worth's poems.
- The young poets may choose who they would like to help enact their poem.

- Follow the same procedure as done with the packet of **Personified Poems**.

NEW HABITS

- After field trips or vacations or a weekend, give students time to write other personifying poems of objects that were particularly memorable.

EXAMPLES

Sunshine

Sunshine
erases
all bad feelings leaving only happiness
until
the rain comes
carrying boredom
and a platter of blue.
Jimmy, 4th grade

Driftwood

Driftwood
a forgotten piece of
memory
soaked by the sea
a faint smell of
low tide
still lingering
smooth as the
night sky
with the occasional
twinkle of stars
a gray-brown mystery
curiosity mingling with hope.
Lili, 5th grade

Baseball Bat

The baseball bat
leaning
against the wall
clumped
among its siblings.

Fingerprints rubbed
permanently
on the bat

The bat charges
the ball
the red seams
on the ball
spinning
to dodge
and charge

The brown bat
tackles
the horrified ball.

                         Ayush, 5th grade

Session 5: BECOMING THE WIND

Materials needed:
- *Copies of the text* How Does The Wind Walk *for every student*
- *Pencil and paper for each student*

WHY THIS SESSION

By using a mentor text, students will reflect on the many attributes of the wind. They will choose one season that has a wind that they are particularly familiar with and write a personifying poem about that wind. Mentor texts can be inspirational and model an approach and a format for a student's poem.

SAY IT

Students, I don't think that there is anything in nature that better lends itself to personifying than the wind. It has so many moods and so many feelings and so many lifelike actions. It grabs people's hats, whips people's skirts, barrels through canyons, and tickles your face with warm fingers. We are going to read a book that gives us a little sampling of the wind's moods and actions during the four seasons. I have passed out your own copy of the text to each of you. I want you to underline it, and write notes to yourself. Make it an important workbook to help give you ideas for your own poem about the wind. I will read the whole book through first and then read it a second time. On the second read-through, I will read each page and then pause to give you time to underline vocabulary that describes the wind's moods, mind, and its personifying action. Let's do the first page all together so you have an idea of what I mean.

SHOW IT

- Read the first page and ask for action words of this fall wind that are usually used with animals or people.
- *Walks with a rush, brushing* and *passes* are all action words used with living beings. These should be underlined. Comment to the students that the way that the boy acts is not personification, but it helps us to get a comparison of a human acting and wind acting in similar ways.
- Now from these action words what is the mood of this wind?
- Point out that it seems very much in a hurry, impatient and rushing.
- It may even be considered irresponsible and not compassionate, because it is knocking leaves off trees and not even stopping to notice.
- Write some of these words on the smartboard or the chart paper.
- Ask the students to write some of these ideas on their activity sheet page.
- They may use these ideas if they choose to write about the fall wind.

DISCOVER IT

- The students will now move ahead at their own pace and with their own ideas and underline any words that help them consider this wind as a person.

NOTE IT

- When you have finished the book, make a chart with two columns titled Action and Mood. Make 4 rows down the side, titled with the names of the four seasons.
- Ask the students to offer examples of action and mood for each season. Use words they have discovered from thinking about and underlining their mentor text.
- When finished with this exercise, the class should have word inspiration for all the seasons.

	Action	Mood
Spring		
Summer		
Fall		
Winter		

BRAVE IT

- Now the students have an opportunity to write their own wind poems.
- Make the chart about the wind, created by the class, available to students looking for some vocabulary inspiration.
- Once the poems are completed, ask the students to draw a picture of the wind that they have personified.

SHARE IT

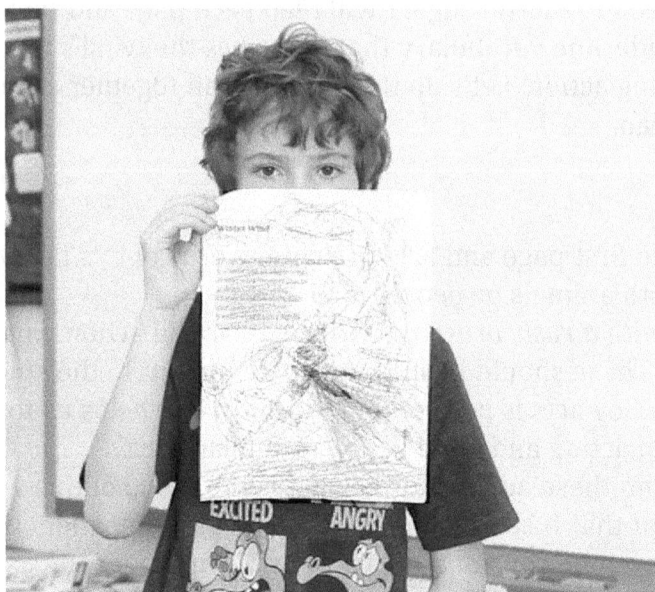

- When the young poets gather, they will read their poems.
- The class will react to the poems as they have to the other personification poems discussing the mood and the action that they can visualize.
- As well, they can share the pictures.

CONTINUE IT

- Have students organize and enact plays of their wind poems.

NEW HABITS

- In the children's nonfiction and fiction writing, begin to look for personification. If it is used, acknowledge it and perhaps even post it.
- In reading circle, notice how authors use personification to communicate their ideas.

Session 6: ANIMALS ARE ALREADY ALIVE

Materials needed:
- *Copy the text of* Twilight Comes Twice *for every student*
- *Pencil and paper for each student*
- *Chart with two columns 1) anthropomorphize; 2) personify*
- *Activity sheet* **Anthropomorphizing and Personifying**

WHY THIS SESSION

By using this mentor text, students will be exposed to a more advanced use of personification. They will be introduced to the vocabulary word *anthropomorphizing* and the fine line that exists between *anthropomorphizing* and *personifying.* Personification is a more effective and creative writing strategy. Making an animal have human characteristics, which is anthropomorphizing, is "cute," but not notable writing.

SAY IT

Students, your well-schooled and disciplined ability to write poetry not only makes you capable poets but as well allows you to be much better writers. A writer's job is to communicate ideas to an audience; using comparisons like you have learned with personification, makes the effort to get your ideas across to others a successful one. Today you are going to learn an important difference between personifying and anthropomorphizing. If you are not careful, your efforts to personify can lose their power and effectiveness. I will write the two words on this chart paper. They are fun words to say and important words to understand if you want to be an advanced writer. The definition of **anthropomorphize** is to give human characteristics to an animal. You make the animal seem like it is a human. You say your dog is bored and needs to go on a vacation. Actually the dog just needs a good walk. He doesn't need to take a plane to Puerto Rico. I anthropomorphize my dogs all the time, because they are my buddies and I like to think of them as people, but it does not mean that they are people. We made the wind seem like a person, we brought it alive, but that is different, and is called **personification**.

We are going to read a book that beautifully communicates to us about the time in the morning and the time in the evening called twilight. Twilight happens twice a day. It happens just as night ends and the morning begins. That is called dawn. And it happens just as the day ends and night begins and that is called dusk.

How many people have noticed the sun at dawn and at dusk? It is just beginning to shine or just ending its shining. Ralph Fletcher, a well-known poet, describes these two times during a day in the text that I have passed out. I am going to read it aloud to you and you are going to see a lot of personifying. You will be able to mark this text like you did with *Where The Wind Walks* but for the first read, just listen and enjoy. When I have finished, I am going to put you into pairs and with your partner you will go through the book and identify all the examples of anthropomorphizing and personifying. Write an "**A**" where you find anthropomorphizing and "**P**" where you find personifying.

SHOW IT

- Pass out copies of the text, *Twilight Comes Twice*.
- Model discovering anthropomorphizing or personifying from the text, for example, explain why "fireflies swim" (page 8 of the text) is anthropomorphizing, and why "night and day whisper secrets" (page 5) is personifying. **1)** A firefly although alive, does not swim like a person. It can only fly. **2)** Night and day are not alive, but seem to come alive by making them whisper.
- Show the class how to note these discoveries with an appropriate **A** and a **P**.
- Do not treat one as bad and another as good; but point out that as a writer, one should know the difference and when which is more effective.
- This may be difficult for the students to understand because most often the lesson is either right or wrong, black or white. This lesson is more subtle awareness of word use and affect.

DISCOVER IT

- Once the students have finished their discovery of anthropomorphizing and personification, give the activity sheet **Anthropomorphizing and Personifying**, to extend and challenge their understanding.
- Do the first examples with them.

NOTE IT

- When the students have finished their discovering, note suggested definitions from the class of these two terms.
- The definitions can be a class synthesis.

BRAVE IT

- Have the students take one of the underlined sentences from the text of *Twilight Comes Twice* or a sentence from the completed

Anthropomorphizing and Personification activity sheets and make it a title of a poem that they will create

- Encourage the students to have fun with their ideas.

CONTINUE IT

- Begin a word wall of personifying and anthropomorphizing. Begin with suggestions like: *My dog told me he loved me. The branch scratched on the window.*
- It will become apparent that it is more difficult to create personifications than it is to create anthropomorphizing. Listen to students beginning to discover that. It shows critical thought.

EXAMPLES OF STUDENTS' WORK

Morning

Rising up
another morning
to the scent of apple crisp.
Looking out my window
Morning mist and dew
lining bushes.
I glimpse a blue bird
Flying overhead.
What a glorious morning

Ella, 4th grade

Dawn

At the break of dawn
dew shimmers and shakes on
the emerald green grass.

Birds call out warning
calls as a fiery colored fox
slinks out of a bristly bush
silent on it's quick light paws.

Squirrels scuttle cautiously
through the underbrush scavenging

A small dappled fawn
steps slowly over a log and
bounds off.
Dew shimmers and shakes
On the emerald green grass
At the break of dawn.

Katya, 4th grade

Session 7: COLOR DOES LIVE

Materials needed:
- *The book* Red Sings from Treetops, *by Joyce Sidman*
- **Taking Notes from *Red Sings from Treetops*** *activity sheet*
- *Pencil and paper and clipboard for each student*
- ***Personify Colors*** *activity sheet*
- *Chart paper for recording discoveries from the book. Note three categories 1.* **Seasonal color;** *2. What is it* **doing**; *3. What* **feeling** *is communicated*

WHY THIS SESSION

By using this mentor text, students will realize that the abstraction of seasons and color can be personified. This mentor text helps the visuals of color and the familiar but elusive attributes of the seasons become tangible. Students will know color and the seasons with a new perspective. They will have greater practice in communicating the abstracts in their life.

SAY IT

Students, we saw how we could bring the wind alive. Now we are going to bring the seasons alive. This poet, Joyce Sidman, used the seasons' colors and made them come alive. I will read it to you and then we will discuss it. As I read, try to visualize those particular colors that come alive in each season. In summer there is a lot more blue and green running around than in winter. The colors that prance around in the winter are primarily black and white. When I finish the first read, I will pass out an activity sheet where we will gather notes about the season's colors. It is from these notes that you will be inspired to write your own season and color poem.

SHOW IT

- Pass out activity sheet **Taking Notes from *Red Sings from Treetops*.**
- Read the stanza about Green in spring and then the Many colors in spring
- Instruct students to underline all the things that green and the many colors can do like a person.
- Together discuss these.
- Choose two or three stanzas from each season in the book by Sidman and read them aloud.
- Pause after each stanza and ask what the **color is doing** and the **feeling that is communicated.**
- On the class chart, note the answers that the students offer and comment on the use of metaphor and personification.
- As the class chart is filled in, the students can fill in their activity sheets.

- For example: the first seasonal color is **red. What is Red doing?** Red is singing and welcoming in new life. **What is the feeling?** It is one of joy and happiness.
- Red also is magical by making **feathery flowers** on branches that were once bare from the winter. This gives a feeling of wonder and awe.

BRAVE IT

- After filling in the activity sheet, **Taking Notes from *Red Sings from Treetops***, hand out the **Personify Colors** activity sheets.
- Together reread the two models of season color personification at the top of the **Taking Notes from *Red Sings from Treetops*** activity sheet
- The Sidman poem stanza focuses on just one color in the spring. The Simmons' poem combines many colors into one stanza.
- Students have the option to use either approach as inspiration.
- Explain that the students are not to copy from the text. Instead they need to decide on their own, their choice of seasonal colors as well as what each color is doing and saying.

SHARE IT

- Have the children share their poems and ask fellow students to comment on the personification and comparisons that are used.
- Discuss what new perspectives were gained from their classmates' poems?

CONTINUE IT

- Enact their season poems.
- Create further season poetry with different colors.
- Draw a picture of one of their personified colors.

NEW HABITS

- Notice colors of clothes or colors on the playground or on a field trip and ask the students what that color might be saying or what mood it casts.

EXAMPLE

In the next poem, a student did not depend on the colors to personify the seasons. She used another approach.

The Seasons

winter
To summer it's midnight while winter roams
To spring it's early but still night
and fall just fell asleep.

spring
Winter is tired as spring comes in
Summer is ready but can wait
Fall is dreaming of red and yellow leaves
While spring is wide awake.

summer
Summer is finally up with hot and sunny days
Fall is starting to prepare the trees
Winter is dreaming of snow and frost
And spring is starting to sleep.

fall
Fall is here with colorful leaves
Winter is getting prepared
Spring dozes peacefully
While summer is falling asleep
Then it starts all over again
Teagon, 4th grade

Name _____

My Letter To:

Write a letter to a familiar **object**

place or

choose a **part of your personality**.

Some Ideas:
1) Tired feet
2) Your good memory
3) Place you lived when you were younger
4) A favorite item of clothing
5) A favorite possession
6) Your patience

Example:

Dear Bed Pillow,

I am writing to let you know how much you mean to me. You are the one that is always there to listen to me when I need someone to listen to me the most. When I lay my head down on your soft, caring lap you let me stay there as long as I want. You absorb my tears so only you and I know that they happened. When I smile you make a cloth wrinkle smile with me.

Thank you for your comfy dependability.

Your friend,

Name _____

FOG

The fog comes
on little cat feet.
It sits looking
over harbor and city
on silent haunches
and then moves on.

Carl Sandberg

Name _____

Personified Poem Acting

- Fill out the worksheet below.
- Now you are ready to **become** your thing and act it out.

What is the character of the object? _____

_____

_____

_____

What words are used to make it act like a human? _____

_____

_____

_____

_____

Have you ever felt or acted like this thing before or known anyone who has?
Do you have a connection with this object? _____

_____

_____

_____

_____

_____

_____

_____

_____

Pencil Sharpener

The sharpener
greedily gobbles
its meal of lead and
wood
digesting and
dumping
the mutilated
pencil remnants
into its silver belly.
Heartlessly its steel teeth
grind away
the simple tool
innocent of its
inevitable end.
Heidi Simmons

Sneakers

Hiding in the closet
Tired
Tongues hanging out
Shoelaces droop
Puddles of burnt rubber
Eyelets flutter
As sleep returns to shoes
Leather retires
Getting ready for the next run.
Joey, 4th grade

Balloon

The balloon slides
silently
through the air
leaving the circus grounds
and gazing into the sun
wagging at an old, big tree
and perching
on a pointy branch
then
POP
erased forever.

Beth, 4th grade

Fence

Wire mesh fingers
intertwine and
and confine
freedom.

Once
space
roamed
forever
but now
never

It bumps
into hard corners
stops,
slumps
and stares
sadly at the other side.

Heidi Simmons

Dahlia bulbs

Each fall
tired bulbs
are tucked away
under blankets
of wood shavings
where they slumber
safely
through the cold winter

until spring
then
green sleepy heads peek
from
the quiet brown ball
soon
to shout loud colors
of summer.

Heidi Simmons

A Table

The table stands proud
polished and
ready to serve

Milk glasses leave
a circle of wet.
Forgotten popsicles
dribble down its leg
into a puddle of
orange.

Book bags are dropped.
Rings of keys clank
heavily
on its back
with disregard.

Until
a large linen square
is snapped spritely
overhead
and smoothed
with ceremony
covering its bruises and abuses
and again
it's ready to serve.

Heidi Simmons

The Sun

How sinister
the sun
to appear
so serene
sashaying sweetly
across the sky
seducing us to bask
in its ravishing rays
and all the while
staining sensitive skin
with sunscald.

Heidi Simmons

Name _____

Anthropomorphizing and Personifying

Below are words to be used in examples of personifying and anthropomorphizing. Two examples are provided to get you started.

> **A**= anthropomorphizing.
>
> **P**= personifying

Wink

> **A:** The dog **winked** at his master and let him know that he understood.
>
> **P:** The sun **winked** away its warmth for a moment as the dark cloud passed over the picnic.

Scowl

> **A:** The horse **scowled** when the small child took a bite out of the apple before it was given to him.
>
> **P:** The cloud **scowled** darkness over the wedding, reminding the bride that she should not marry the groom.

Smile

> **A:** _____
>
> _____
>
> _____
>
> **P:** _____
>
> _____
>
> _____

Whisper

> **A:** _____
>
> _____
>
> _____
>
> **P:** _____
>
> _____
>
> _____

Name _____

Sing

     A: _____

       _____

       _____

     P: _____

       _____

       _____

Pout

     A: _____

       _____

       _____

     P: _____

       _____

       _____

Cry

     A: _____

       _____

       _____

     P: _____

       _____

       _____

Blush

     A: _____

       _____

       _____

     P: _____

       _____

       _____

Name _____

Punch

    A: _____

        _____

        _____

    P: _____

        _____

        _____

Hug

    A: _____

        _____

        _____

    P: _____

        _____

        _____

Name _____

Personify Colors and extend them into a poem

1. Choose your favorite season _____
2. When you think of that season, what are the 2 or 3 colors that YOU see most clearly during that season?

Where in this season do you see the 1st color?

I see it in _____

_____

_____

What is it doing or saying _____

_____

_____

What feeling is communicated _____

_____

_____

Where in this season do you see the 2nd color?

I see it in_____

_____

_____

What is it doing or saying _____

_____

_____

What feeling is communicated _____

_____

_____

Name _____

Where in this season do you see the 3rd color?

I see it in _____

_____

_____

What is it doing or saying _____

_____

_____

What feeling is communicated _____

_____

_____

3. Having gathered these ideas, write your personification - of - color poem.

_____

_____

_____

_____

_____

_____

_____

_____

_____

_____

_____

Name _____

Models of Personifying Season's Color

Green in spring

Green is new
in spring. Shy
green peeks
from buds,
trembles on the breeze.
Green floats through the rain-dark trees
and glows, mossy-soft at my feet
Green drips from tips of leaves
onto the pup's nose.
In spring
even the rain tastes **green.**

Joyce Sidman

Many Colors in spring

In spring, **blue** spreads out her blanket
for y**ellow** to lie and bask in its warmth.
White puffs laze along the sky
until BOOM! **White** rips a jagged line across the stormy **black.**
Green is first to pop up through winter **brown.**
New **green** tickles the ants' feet.
Green stands straight and tall swinging the daffodil's **yellow** cup
    in the breeze.

Heidi Simmons

Name _____

SEASONAL COLOR	WHAT IS IT DOING	WHAT IS THE FEELING
spring red	Singing and welcoming in new life	There is a feeling of joy and happiness
spring red	Magically making feathery flowers on bare branches	There is a feeling of wonder and awe

Name _____

SEASONAL COLOR	WHAT IS IT DOING	WHAT IS THE FEELING

Name _____

SEASONAL COLOR	WHAT IS IT DOING	WHAT IS THE FEELING

✦ Lesson 7: Image and Comparison: Metaphor, Simile, and Personification

Explicit **Poetic Element Instruction:** Image and Comparison
Implied **Poetic Element Learning:** Choosing the right word; Rhythm; Heart and Message;

WHY THIS LESSON

Two ways of using comparison that further the student's word competency are *simile* and *metaphor*. With these comparisons a student's word usage reaches new heights. As previously noted, the art of metaphor and simile comes naturally to humans. Researchers have found that children understand metaphors as early as age two. This lesson will help students move beyond unwitting use of metaphor into consciously creating their own.

To be effective, this lesson requires time and practice. Students can scale great heights in word usage and understanding when they are able to internalize the concepts and move at their own pace. It can be difficult to find enough time and patience in the twenty-first century classroom to allow young students to ascend to their potential heights. Nonetheless, given the opportunity, young minds are supple and athletic and can climb beautifully.

Session 1: BEYOND PERSONIFYING

Materials needed:
- *Suggested Similes Chart prepared ahead of class time (see* **Suggested Similes** *section)*
- *Chart of simile to metaphor examples in* ***AGAIN SAY IT*** *section*
- **Changing Simile to Metaphor** *activity sheet*

WHY THIS SESSION

The students will begin to understand the difference between a simile and a metaphor. With this knowledge they can begin also to understand how a metaphor evolves in the mind and on paper.

SAY IT

You now have experience with comparing the inanimate, (not alive) world to the live world. The wind knocked at windows, spring sang, the color green was shy, the fog slunk along like a little cat, and pencil sharpeners were gobbling up pencils.

Comparisons help us communicate how we see the world, by bringing things alive and showing us new ways to imagine. Now we are going to learn two other ways to compare and communicate ideas, through the use of simile and metaphor. By comparing something to something else, the reader gets a clearer mental picture of the idea that a writer wants to communicate.

For example, if I say, "I feel full," you have no idea how full I really am until I compare it to something. If instead, I said, "I am so full, I feel like a blown up balloon," you get an image clear enough to draw on paper. If I say that someone is thin, you are left to wonder how thin. If I say, "He is so thin he could slip under a door," you can imagine that this person is too thin to be real and smile at the thought of it. Now I would like you to create some clear images in my head by using similes. I want you to get into pairs. I have written some beginning comparisons on the chart.

See how many creative similes you can create. You do not have to write the whole sentence, just the created simile.

SUGGESTED SIMILES

- The day is as hot as…
- His serving of ice cream was as big as…
- The new waxed floor was as slippery as…
- When he jumped out from behind the chair, I screamed like…
- I was not happy. The piece of candy he offered me was as small as…
- His smile was as wide as…
- She was so excited that she jumped up and down like…
- She is a fast runner. She runs like a…
- He does nothing. He just sits around the house like a…
- She is very shy and always quiet as a… (do not say mouse)

SHARE IT

- As always with student creations, share them in the writing circle.
- Have fellow students comment on the images that are created by the similes.
- At the end ask why you did not want them to use the simile, "quiet as a mouse."
- If necessary, explain that a mouse is what everyone usually compares quiet to and the students' goal is to create new ideas of comparison.

AGAIN SAY IT

A simile helps us to get to a metaphor. A metaphor starts with an image like a simile does, but then, without saying exactly what we are comparing something to, we use description words that give enough of a hint a reader knows what is being used for a comparison.

Chart the simile to metaphor examples, in bold print below, so the students can visualize as well as listen to the differentiating explanation.

If I want to change the simile "**his cheeks are red like cherries**," to a metaphor, I might say, "**His cheeks were bright red and shiny from the heat of the fire**." I didn't say cherry, I just said bright red and shiny.

If I want to change the simile "**he ran as fast as a horse**," to a metaphor, I could say, "**He bolted across the starting line and galloped toward the finish line. He pounded along through the dirt and clouds of dust rose up around his legs**." The runner has been compared to a horse but a horse was not mentioned. What is so cool about metaphors is that the reader can think that you are talking about a zebra or a gazelle, an antelope, or whatever animal is most familiar to them that acts like that, but the message is the same: The kid runs fast, really fast.

I am going to give you an activity sheet that will help you to understand the difference between similes and metaphors. You will change the similes to metaphors and then when we have finished, propose your own definition of a metaphor and a simile.

SHOW IT

- Take out the activity sheet **Changing Simile to Metaphor**.
- Go over the examples in the activity sheet. The *like* or *as* in a simile and not in a metaphor can be noted but should not be the only observed difference.
- After they do the exercise, ask them to explain the differences themselves.
- Let the students lead the understanding.

DISCOVER IT

- A choice of a partner can be helpful for a new and challenging exercise.
- It is important when the students are working on this activity sheet that they have time to explore their own understanding. This is a pivotal moment in their poetry and language advancement.

NOTE IT

- When the students have finished their activity sheets, bring them back to the writing circle and have them share their responses.
- With each response, ask fellow classmates if the simile has become a metaphor and how.
- They might make personifications instead of metaphors, e.g.: *"His words were like a sword. The words stabbed me and bled my soul."* If this happens, point it out, while supporting it as a successful effort of expanding on the simile. It is comparison and that is, after all, exactly what a metaphor is.

- When they have finished this exercise, have them return to their pairs and try to create definitions for simile and metaphor.
- Create final definitions that reflect a cooperative effort made up of several sentences from several students.
- Hang these definitions up on the wall for a few weeks.

CONTINUE IT

- Have the children take out their independent reading books and read for at least half an hour, armed with sticky notes. If they find a simile, metaphor, or personification, have them note it and share it with the class later.
- As they share their findings, ask them to identify which comparison their findings are: simile, metaphor, or personification.

NEW HABITS

- Have a stack of index cards near a pin board or blank wall. Each morning have the children check in with an example of a comparison from their last night's reading.
- Share the findings at morning meeting, just before going home, or other open moments.

Session 2: COMMUNICATING WITH COMPARISONS

Materials needed:

- *Prepared chart of SCIENCE TO METAPHOR explained in* **SHOW IT**
- **Change Science to Metaphor** *activity sheet*

WHY THIS SESSION

Young children's interaction with the world is primarily through the five senses. The world is communicated through their touch, sight, hearing, smell and taste. Language development is critical to a writer's ability to communicate that world.

The poem below, written by a fifth grade student, exemplifies the sensorial focus of young students. Although she clearly still has one foot in her young world of the five senses, she is moving into a more challenging world of the abstract through the use of metaphor, for example, comparing the feel of poetry to a corduroy jacket or its appearance to a chubby orange crayon. That which is a challenge to comprehend or difficult to define to a child, can become comprehensible and definable through metaphor. For example, children do not always have the scientific terminology for observed scientific phenomenon.

Because students may be unfamiliar with the scientific terminology, they may have difficulty communicating what they have observed.

In this session, students will practice using metaphor, personification, and simile to communicate scientific phenomena.

Poetry

Poetry **feels** like a corduroy jacket
or a rust brass button.
Poetry **sounds** like the moon whispering the truth,
true north, good truth.
Not like the poisonous lies which sometimes
seep into your heart.
We know it happens.
Poetry **looks** like
my chubby orange crayon
dull at the tip that hides under the floral print cushion
of my old doll chair.
Poetry **tastes** like summer, the honey dribbling down my chin.
Poetry **smells** like a lavender wand, with a drape of fresh Penelope.
Poetry kisses you, hugs you in a warm embrace.
                    Emma, 5th grade

SAY IT

We have seen that by using comparisons like simile, personification, and metaphor, we are able to communicate ideas in a way that we and our readers can clearly see. That gives us a lot of power. One thing that is sometimes difficult for people to communicate is scientific observation because, although they can sense it, they do not know the scientific words to explain it. When we feel the warmth of the sun, we do not usually communicate in a scientific way and say, "Oh, there is our nearest star. The warmth of its fiery gases, most of which are hydrogen, feels nice." We can communicate our feelings about the sun more clearly with a metaphor. We might say, "The sun blanketed its warmth around my shivering body." When you say that, you have successfully communicated with me. I know exactly how cozy the sun makes you feel. I know that you have experienced warm blankets just like I have so there is a connection between us. And I can see the idea that you have in your head because you have used words that clearly describe that image. So a metaphor can be useful as a substitute for unfamiliar scientific terms.

What we are going to practice today is taking scientific descriptions that use words that are not familiar to our everyday language, and transforming them with metaphors and personification, into language that is familiar and communicates a clear, understandable image.

SHOW IT

- Create a chart of SCIENCE TO METAPHOR. Write down examples 1, 1a, 2, 2a.

1) Snow forms when the atmospheric temperature is at or below freezing (0 degrees Celsius or 32 degrees Fahrenheit) and there is a minimum amount of moisture in the air. If the ground temperature is at or below freezing, the snow will remain on the ground. However, the snow can still reach the ground when the ground temperature is above freezing.

Explain to the students that this is factually correct, but one does not get a very clear image of what is happening. Changing it to metaphoric language will give a clearer, more familiar image.

1a) Outside was a veil of wintery white. Inside we snuggled in the warm cocoons of our comforters.

Discuss which sentences about snow give you a clear image about snow and how snow impacts on you.

2) The sun is our nearest star. It is composed of hot fiery gases most of which are hydrogen.

Again, explain to the students that this is factually correct, but one does not get a clear image or heartfelt feeling for what is happening. Changing it to metaphoric language will give a clearer, more familiar image.

2a) The sun's warmth wrapped around the shivering child. She was then quieted.

Discuss which sentences about the sun give a clearer image and how the sun impacts on everyday life.

DISCOVER IT

- Hand out the **Change Science to Poetry** activity sheets.
- A choice of a partner can be helpful for a new and challenging exercise.

NOTE IT

- When the students have finished their activity sheets, bring them back to the writing circle and have them share their responses.
- With each response, ask fellow classmates what image they now have about the scientific statement.
- When they have finished, ask the students to explain what the scientific sentences did for them as well the poetic sentences.

- Students draw pictures of their own or others' metaphoric sentences.

CONTINUE IT

- Use the metaphoric sentences created from the scientific sentences as the beginning of a poem.
- Each student takes three main words from the sentences they have created and makes them a title of a poem.
- During science, take a scientific fact and challenge the class to make a metaphor or personification to make it a clearer image in the class's mind.

NEW HABITS

- When explaining or clarifying something in class, practice using a metaphor or personification yourself. Note that you have done it, so that the students can see the usefulness of the figure of speech.

EXAMPLES

1. Earthworms can be cut in half and do not die. Instead they grow the part that is missing and continue their life.

   - *Cut in half, yet still alive squirming around. One half blind, the other in pain, missing its other side.*
     Allison, 5th grade

2. Snow is a form of precipitation within the Earth's atmosphere in the form of crystalline water ice, consisting of snowflakes that fall from clouds.

   - *The cold winter breeze danced on my face and I froze like an iceberg.*
     Sequoia, 5th grade

   - *Frosty fingers cast a frozen spell upon the outside world.* Lily, 5th grade

3. The sun is the star at the center of the solar system. It consists of hot plasma interwoven with magnetic fields.

   - *The sun like a huge fiery ball waltzes with us.*
     Josh, 5th grade

Session 3: VENN DIAGRAMS DECIDE

Materials needed:
- **Venn Diagram** *template activity sheet*
- **Poems for The Venn Diagram** *activity sheet*
- *Prepare a chart of three Venn diagrams with the comparisons of the three poems noted (see* **SHOW IT***).*

WHY THIS SESSION

Students use comparisons to find meaning in the world as well as make the world meaningful in new ways to readers. Similes with deep comparisons are the beginning of successful metaphoric or personifying poems. In this session, the students will learn to use a Venn diagram to assess the depth of a comparison and the potential success of creating a metaphoric and personifying poem.

SAY IT

We are going to continue with our exploration of comparisons and how to use them to explain how we see our world as well as help others see the world with greater imagination and interest. I want to remind you of a book we read a while ago. You can see the rewards of using good comparisons. They inspire our imagination and we feel like we are experiencing this owling adventure. I will read you the book and when you hear a comparison that helps you to see the experience, raise your hand. The comparisons we make as poets are not particularly rewarding to us or to our readers unless the comparisons we make are deep and imaginative like in the poem *Owl Moon* that we read in Lesson 3.

So how do we measure if a comparison is deep? Today we will use a Venn Diagram to measure how much two ideas we are comparing have in common. Let's begin with a simile: **the moon is like a rubber ball,** and test if that is a deep comparison. [*Draw a Venn diagram and write the word **rubber ball** in one edge of one intersecting circle and the word **moon** in the other edge. In the common intersecting space, write **round**. Under **ball**, note its characteristics that are not common to the moon:* rubber, bouncy, playground equipment; *and then, under moon, note its characteristics that are not common to a ball's:* a satellite, rotates with the earth, a celestial object.] One can see by this diagram that it is difficult to find anything deeper in our comparison but that they are round. That does not make a successful poem or an enlightening comparison for the writer or the reader.

Let's try another one: **My sister is like a puppy**. [*Make the Venn diagram and put puppy in one circle and sister in the other circle.*] Let's think about a puppy. It has floppy ears, a furry face, a licking tongue, playful. [*Place all these attributes under the "puppy" in the Venn diagram.*] Now, let's think about a sister. She has floppy hair, not ears or fur. She reads books. She is playful. *[Place all these attributes under the "sister" in the Venn diagram.]* We have found one commonality to put in the center, *"playful."* Is that hopeful for a successful poem? My sister is playful like a puppy... but then where do we go?

What if I said, **the icicle was like a candy cane.** This time, I want you to make a Venn Diagram with that comparison and tell me if it has the depth of comparison to be a good poem. *[Allow the students to work on a Venn diagram comparing these two. If they only propose that both are long and skinny, that will not make a deep metaphor poem. But if they can go further, then they are on their way to a great poem.]*

We are going to study metaphor through poetry. We will look at three poems and judge whether or not they are deep, imaginative comparisons by using a Venn diagram.

SHOW IT

- Give the students **Poems for The Venn Diagram** activity sheet.
- Pass out Venn diagram templates.
- Get into pairs and place each poem in a Venn Diagram.
- You can tell the success and depth of a poem by the number of creative commonalities the two items that you are comparing have.
- To get the students started, discuss what is being compared in each poem
- There is the moon and a father; and the poetry and a sugar–crazed teenager.
- Have the students note these comparisons on three of the Venn diagrams.
- Begin by talking about the moon and a daddy.
- The moon takes care of the sun and a daddy takes care of a son so that goes in the common middle.
- These poem examples are a mixture of personification and metaphor.
- You are searching for clever comparisons so either effort can work.

DISCOVER IT

- Have the students fill in the rest of the commonalities for MOON and complete the activity sheets on the poem POETRY.
- Those students who finish ahead of others can begin to take the common elements of the compared ideas and start to write their own poem on comparing a moon to a parent or a poem to a sugar-crazed teenager.

NOTE IT

- When the students have finished their activity sheets, bring them back to the writing circle and demonstrate the charting of the Venn diagrams by the students' suggestions.

BRAVE IT

- Instruct the children to make the language in the common center of the Venn diagram.
- Choose one of the Venn diagram centers to inspire the writing of a class poem.
- If needed, use the example below to scaffold class thinking (The poem is inspired from the Venn Diagram poem, *Moon*).

EXAMPLE

The moon
A father to the sun
waits patiently
until,
his boy
fatigued with
brightening the earth
all day
is ready to be tucked away
into the horizon.
And as he sleeps
the moon begins
his fatherly vigil.

Heidi Simmons

CONTINUE IT

- Find other metaphor poems in your poetry books and have the students create Venn diagrams as proof of the depth of the metaphors used in the poems.

NEW HABITS

- When students find comparisons in their reading, give the comparisons the Venn diagram test to assess whether or not the poet has been successful in the comparison.

Session 4: KEEN COMPARISONS

Materials needed:

- *Charted categories of positive feelings: Safe, Happy, Empowered, Confident, Special, Creative, Inspired*
- *Paper and pencil*
- *Activity sheet* **From Simile to Especially**

WHY THIS SESSION

Metaphors and personification can make the unfamiliar ideas like: 1) what does 32 degrees look like; and 2) what can hot plasma interwoven with magnetic fields feel like; or 3) what is it like to be in the middle of a crystalline water ice storm, become familiar to us. We have also seen how metaphors and personification can make the familiar even more fabulous through unique comparisons. Remember the personified poems in **Lesson 6, Session 4** that were enacted and then created. They made the everyday world around us suddenly have new meaning. For children, poetry gives meaning to both the familiar and the unfamiliar in their world. They gain a unique understanding through creative use of language. In this session, the students will use collected commonalities to write a poem to gain and communicate new understanding of things important in their world.

SAY IT

Students, today you are going to create metaphors and personification to help understand something important in your world. To help you think of ideas, I have created categories. Think of things that you see, hear, touch, taste, or smell that can give you these feelings that I have charted. What are things that make you feel: *Safe, Happy, Empowered, Confident, Special, Creative, Inspired?*

Let me give you some examples. I will write them below the appropriate column. A mom's hug makes you feel **safe;** or standing in the top of a tree may **empower** you; or hearing the welcoming bark of your dog makes you **happy;** or seeing a sunset might **inspire** you to paint; or maybe a father's bedtime story may make you feel **special.** We will go around the circle once and list your ideas in the categories and as others give their thoughts, it might help you think of more ideas.

SHOW IT

- Once these ideas are on the chart, hand out the activity sheets and lead the class through the first step of choosing the especially important thing from the list on the chart or one that they have thought of on their own.
- Before they start, read the examples that other students have written that are at the end of this session. They are comparisons of important things that other students their age have made. These are poems. Students can also write a paragraph.

- Point out the variety of choices of things that can be important to a person.
- Ask them if they think that the comparisons are deep. Why or why not?
- Emphasize the new way that we now have for looking at something and ask if they think that the young poets were pleased with their poems.
- Give them the activity sheet **From Simile to Especially**.

BRAVE IT

- Encourage the students to accomplish this task on their own. How willing and enthusiastic they are to tackle this challenge will be a measure of their understanding and competency in creating and recognizing personification and metaphor.
- Students who are struggling may need help in creating their Venn diagram.
- Help them decide if the comparison is deep, then encourage them to write their own poem or paragraph.
- Throughout the exercise, ask the members of the class to share their progress. It can motivate others and inspire ideas.

SHARE IT

- Gather in the writing circle for the read-aloud.
- With each reading draw a Venn diagram and as the students read, fill it in.
- Discuss what each child particularly liked about the poems that were read.

CONTINUE IT

- Have the students illustrate their writing, creatively combining the comparisons into an image.
- Display these illustrations.

NEW HABITS

- Similar to the last session, have the students continue to find comparisons in their reading. Give the comparisons the Venn diagram test to assess whether or not the poet has made a "deep" comparison.

EXAMPLES

The Ornamental Moon Of Xmas (compares a *special* xmas ornament to the moon)

An ornate sphere
glowing butter yellow
in the quiet of the night
in the bright reflected light.

Hanging
suspended in the air
slowly drifting
across the darkened sky

leaving a trail
of shimmering stars
illuminating the mysterious

Rejoicing in the beginning of its reign
adorning
its domain
basking in its short time of glory
only to be tucked away again.
Elleanora, 5th grade

Emotional Weather (compares *emotion* to the weather)

A storm of emotions
testing a friendship's
survival.

A bright emotion
making it a lovely fun day
after a downpour of gray
sadness.

A hurricane of feelings
making a fun beginning
into "a horrible, no good, very bad day"

A sun of joy
warms the depressed hearts
of failed friendships

Emotion is like weather
uncontrollable
testing
and unpredictable.
Allyson, 5th grade

POETRY and OCEAN (compares the *ocean* to poetry)

Both deep
with meaning.
The deep sea creatures
live in the murky depths of the ocean.
The words of meaning
live in poems.
Each wave
in the ocean
is a crashing thought.
Lucas, 4th grade

Pencil (compares *pencil writing on paper* to snake)

A lead snake
Slithering across the blank paper
Giving it a life
So therefore the pencil is nothing with out a
Paper
a lifeless mineral
that is not there.
Baxter, 4th grade

As Twilight Descends (compares *twilight* to a blanket)

A blanket of black
and navy blue
covers the drowsy sun
a far away wind
brings in the stars
and the night sky
hangs up the moon.
Meg, 5th grade

Session 5: VISUALIZE THE INVISIBLE

Materials needed:
- **Visualizing the Invisible** *activity sheets*
- *A basket of "concrete" objects for possible comparisons for the concepts. A list of suggested objects is in the* **Show It** *section of this lesson.*

WHY THIS SESSION

The metaphor gives young students the opportunity to understand the world on their terms. Abstract concepts like love, hate, courage, loneliness, fear, pride are elusive to young children who primarily are practiced in the concrete world use a viewing lens through their senses. There are dictionary descriptions of these concepts but those are someone else's words, someone else's interpretation. This session shows students how to perceive the abstract as useful and meaningful to their lives.

In the introduction to this book, *Words On Fire*, a young student was referenced concerning her search for comprehending the abstract concept of "disillusionment." Through her trained word awareness development, she concluded that to be disillusioned was when "your eyes were bigger than the stomach of the world." She made the metaphoric connection from her concrete world of asking for too much ice cream to expecting too much of life. Only a metaphor connecting with her familiar concrete world could give her a visual of the otherwise invisible concept, "disillusionment." In this session, the students will connect abstract concepts to their familiar concrete world, which in turn will empower their language control and abstract conceptual awareness.

SAY IT

Students, today we are going to think about words that we use often, but can be difficult to define. You hear war is bad, bullying is not right, arguments are uncomfortable, control freaks aren't fun to play with. But really what is war, bullying, arguments, control? I would struggle to tell you my description. Could you tell me your description? The best way to describe concepts that we cannot see or touch, is to make them touchable and visible. Listen to how a child your age described the word frustration. She makes a comparison to a starved lion. Now she, the writer, knows what she means by frustration and I, the reader, have a new vision of what frustration might entail.

Frustration

It feasts on my brain
like a starved lion
tracking
a group of gazelles.
Numbers
and letters shooting
at my head
and tearing my brain cells.
Staring at a blank
empty
page.
Tears of frustration
rain down
and
a page remains
white
empty page
nothing
all nothing.

Mary, 4th grade

Can you now **see** frustration? Feel its unfriendly ways? Recognize it when those sharp teeth begin to gnaw on the brain? Maybe now that Mary has given us this connection, we have a better understanding of what frustration is. Then, perhaps we can recognize it and once we do that, even control it. Comparisons help us to feel the things in our world that we cannot see. Once we get a feeling for them we can walk up to them and begin to deal with them. We can walk up to frustration and say, "Hey frustration, there you are again, chewing away at my brain and making it difficult for me to go on. Well get out of the way, because I need to move on." I am going to give you an opportunity to visualize some abstract concepts, and explore new understanding of them as Mary did. I will give you a list of abstract concepts and we can talk about other ones that you might like to add. I have a basket here of concrete objects that may be useful for finding or making comparisons. Understand that you can have your own suggestions for concepts and your own ideas for concrete comparisons. These are just to get that brain in creation mode.

SHOW IT

- Hand out the activity sheet **Visualizing the Invisible.**
- Have the children do their own activity sheets. The willingness to take on the task independently is an assessment of their confidence and competence of this lesson's objective.

- Read the directions to the activity sheet and explain that the meaning of metaphor and personification can help us to understand and control life by giving it language as Mary did.
- There are other examples below from students that have done this exercise.
- Use them at any time for further motivation. Sometimes too many examples can stifle individual creativity. Trust yourself to make that call.
- The basket of items that you share can have items like: band-aids, rubber ball, a pen, bottle of water, sugar, a book, white-out, paintbrush, lipstick, napkin, scissors, etc. Inventory your home and gather items in the basket that have applicable comparative attributes to the concepts on the list.
- Before the students begin their effort, give them an opportunity to suggest new concepts that have occurred to them. Be sure too, that they feel free to make a comparison with a concrete object not in the basket.
- Have Venn diagram sheets available for students who may need them but be aware that too much organization can be used as a work-avoidance tactic. Do not offer so much scaffolding that it can be used as an excuse not to write.

BRAVE IT

- Throughout the exercise, ask members of the class to share their progress with the rest of the class. It can motivate others and inspire their ideas.
- If students are struggling, the teacher can give them some comparative ideas or set up a Venn Diagram with them to decide if the comparison is deep while giving them enough help to continue.

SHARE IT

- Gather in the writing circle for the read-aloud.
- With each reading, chart and emphasize the comparisons.
- Discuss what each child particularly liked about the poems that were read.
- After **BRAVE IT** the students proudly share their work.

CONTINUE IT

- Have the students illustrate the images created in their poems and display them.
- Make **Visualizing the Invisible**, a station or an option during guided reading.
- Create a class book of **Understanding the World** or a book of a similar title from the collection of all the class's creations.

NEW HABITS

- During guided reading, if an abstract concept is read, challenge the students to compare it to a concrete object.
- Keep a collection of these discoveries on index cards on a pin board near the reading area.

EXAMPLES

Sadness (*the concept sadness compared to a wrinkled shirt*)

Silence, only the sound
of sadness
like a wrinkled shirt
that fell off its hanger.
You want the day
just to be over.
One disappointment
after another.
Finally sleep
overpowers
and
happiness is born.

Lili, 4th grade

A Band Aid Of Apology (*the concept of apology compared to a band aid*)

A band aid is an apology
concealing the painful marks
smoothing them away
beneath the comfy pad
in a heart to heart conversation
together healing
your inside
throughout.
The band aid
clear, soft and accepting,
leaving you with a warm feeling
never bent, crumpled or blinded
while still
leaving the scars of the past
in existence.

Fritz, 5th grade

Apology Cleansing (*the concept of apology compared to a disinfectant*)

An apology wipes
clean the injury
of an argument.
Helps to
heal
the injury of
hate.
Disinfects
the wounds
of
a verbal
war
helps everyone
and you
by ridding
the room
of
disease
and
injury.

Josh, 5th grade

The Imagination Flower (*the concept of imagination compared to a flower*)

Like a flower
imagination
is planted permanently as
a seed
in your
dirt mind.
The idea sprouts
growing a strong thought-stem.
Budding and flowering
as new ideas are formed
added to the strong
tall standing
growing
'imaginaflower.'

Meg, 5th grade

War (*The concept of war compared to a plane*)

War is a plane
flying across the sky of peace
carrying people from all over the planet
and dropping people all over the planet
then landing
on the runway of peace
and ending
but not for long
then taking off
and flying
again.

> Ian, 5th grade

Courage

What is courage?
A golden sunrise
shining through darkness
to make it go away.

What is courage?
A river slicing through
the country side
swishing and splashing
onto the grass.

What is courage?
Spring popping out
taking winter away
with colorful flowers.

What is courage?
A protecting mother bird
guarding her baby
so it can be safe

What is courage?
Red hearts that
make someone else
to help you
when you need help.

> Leyonce, 3rd grade

Name _____

Changing Simile to Metaphor

Examples:

Simile: The sun was LIKE a big yellow balloon.

Metaphor: The sun floated over us throughout the day, quietly drifting through a sea of blue. It hit the horizon and popped and disappeared into darkness.

Simile: His words were LIKE a sword.

Metaphor: His words were pointed and sharp. Inside, I cried with the pain. The wound they made would never heal.

CHANGE THESE SIMILES BELOW INTO METAPHORS:

He was **as** courageous **as** a lion._____

_____

_____

She was angry **like** a mad bull._____

_____

_____

His self-confidence was **as** big **as** a mountain. _____

_____

_____

She ate her spaghetti **like** a pig._____

_____

_____

Name _____

Change Science to Metaphor

1. Earthworms can be cut in half and do not die. Instead they grow the part that is missing and continue their life.

   _____
   _____
   _____
   _____

2. The moon makes a complete orbit around the earth every 27.3 days.

   _____
   _____
   _____
   _____

3. Snow is a form of precipitation within the Earth's atmosphere in the form of crystalline water ice, consisting of snowflakes that fall from clouds.

   _____
   _____
   _____
   _____

4. The sun is the star at the center of the solar system. It consists of hot plasma interwoven with magnetic fields.

   _____
   _____
   _____
   _____

Name _____

Poems For The Venn Diagram

POETRY

Poetry is like some
sugar-crazed teenager
who just got a license
but refuses to follow
the rules of the road.

It races out of control
then jams up the traffic by
going reeeeeaaaalll slooooooooooow.
It turns up the music so loud
you can't sleep at night.
I can't figure out how it Decides
to capitalize certain Words
Punctuation ? Ha! A joke!
Won't use complete sentences

And why does it refuse to
      stay
           on
               the
                   line?
The most annoying thing?
Poetry won't shut up.
It embarrasses everyone
by telling the truth.

                by Ralph Fletcher

THE MOON

The Moon is a Daddy
to the sun
SO when the moon has tucked in the sun
for tonight
and kisses his sun
and says sleep tight
the moon takes over
his son's place
He holds the sky.

Venn Diagram, 2 Circles

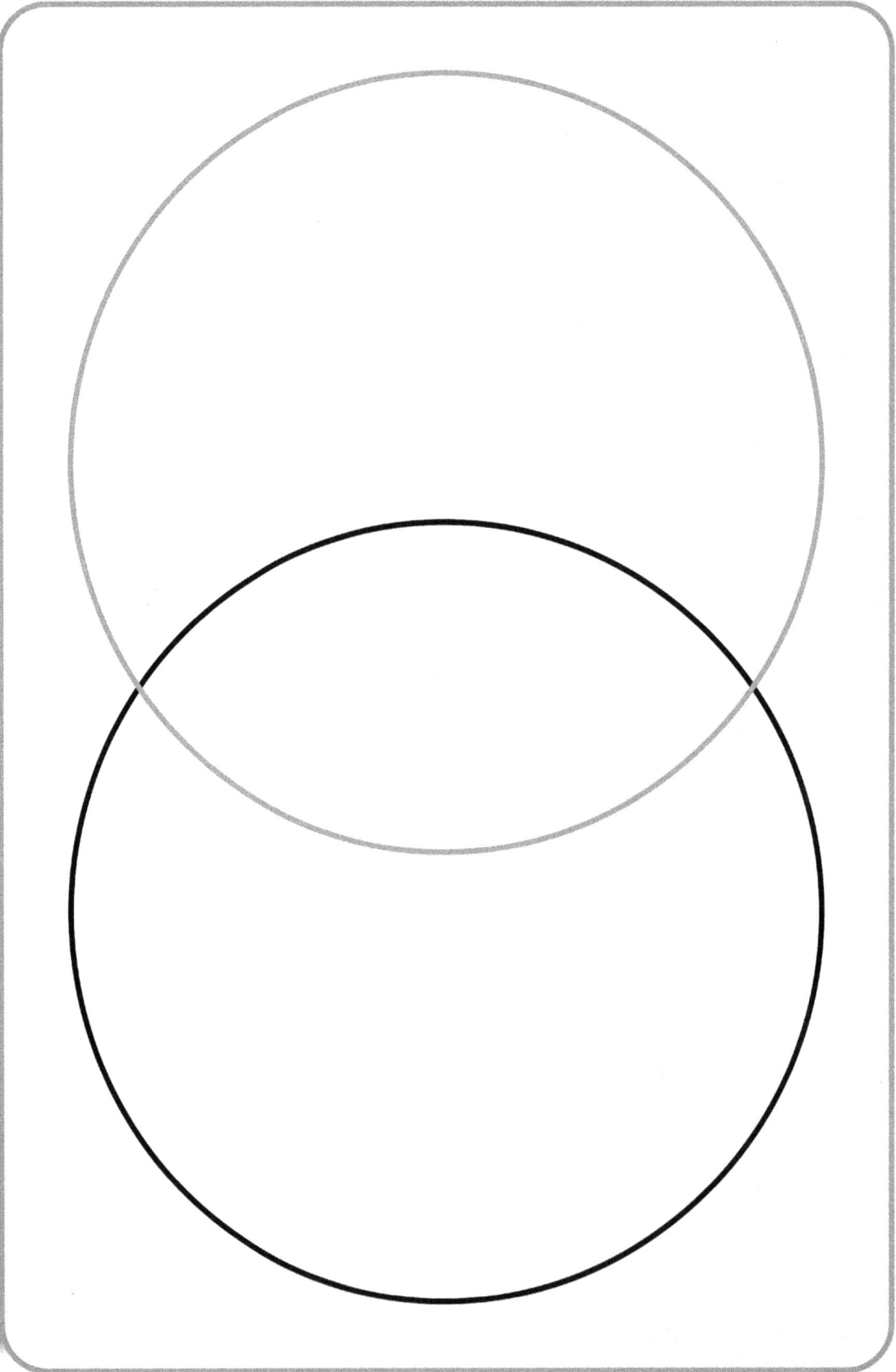

WORDS ON FIRE, © 2017, Heidi Simmons
All Rights Reserved.

Name _____

From Simile To Especially

Write below what you have chosen that is **especially** important to you:

_____IS LIKE_____

_____

Fill in the blanks with what you can **compare** it to that will help you and a reader understand how you feel toward and think about your important feeling or thing:

Fill out a Venn Diagram to see how deep a comparison your simile is.

_____IS LIKE_____

_____

If you only have one or two things listed as similarities in the middle of your diagram, either **create a new simile** or **pick a new important thing**, to make a simile that has more depth.

A Second Time:

Write below what you have chosen that is **especially** important to you:

_____

Fill in the blanks with what you can **compare** it to that will help you and a reader understand how you feel toward and think about your important feeling or thing:

_____IS LIKE_____

_____

Name _____

Visualizing the Invisible

Choose one of the concepts below with which you have some experience or understanding. Choose one of the items in the basket or something else you are familiar with, to use to compare to the concept to make a metaphor.

Your goal is to communicate to us what your opinion, feeling, and/or understanding is about the concept by comparing it to an object. **Metaphor** and **personification** help us to understand and control life by giving it language.

Choice of concepts:
- War
- Happiness
- Love
- Time
- An idea
- Health
- An argument
- Learning
- Control
- Anger
- Bullying
- Writing
- Friendship
- An apology
- Imagination

Name _____

Visualizing the Invisible

Write the concept you have chosen on the line below.

Concept_____

Choose an item from the basket, or your own idea, that is like the concept and can help you explain what your feelings are about this concept.

The concept_____is like_____

because_____

_____

_____

Choose an item from the basket that is **NOT LIKE** the concept and can help you to explain what your feelings are about this concept.

The concept _____is not like_____

because_____

_____

_____

✦ Lesson 8: Form, Strategy, and Teacher Creativity

Explicit Implicit **Poetry Element Instruction:** Image and Comparison; Choosing the right word; Rhythm; Heart and Message

WHY THIS LESSON

Lesson 8 assumes that Lessons 1-7 have provided a foundation for word awareness and poetry acquisition. The young student now has greater independence and confidence, providing the freedom and ability to branch off into more creative exercises.

SESSION ORGANIZATION

Lesson 8 is still organized in sessions but instruction is no longer organized in the Consistent Process. In this lesson, the student is inspired from poetic forms and strategies including Ode, Haiku, Cinquain, Alliteration, Assonance, Consonance, and Onomatopoeia. The instructional approach and creative use of available resources will depend on the unique pedagogy of each teacher.

Each session is organized with:
- **Materials needed** (when applicable beyond pencil and paper)
- **DESCRIPTION**
- **EXAMPLES**
- **ACTIVITY SHEET** (If needed. EXAMPLES are often enough direction for students practiced in poetic expression.)
- **EXTENDED BIBLIOGRAPHY**

Session 1: ODE

Materials needed:
- *Pencil and paper*
- *Examples from Pablo Neruda's book of odes referenced in the bibliography.*

DESCRIPTION

The ode is a dedication to one dignified subject. Throughout the ode, the poet creates verse that rises and falls with emotional intensity. The goal is to make the subject that the poet chooses to appear noble, splendid, important and regal. The poet does this through verse that praises and shows adoration of the object, person, or animal.

EXAMPLES

Ode to a pencil

The page is
blank
A bank of virgin
snow
untouched
unseen
seamless stretches
of remarkable
purity
and then
a mark
mars the immaculate.
Marching steps of grey scribble
skipping rhythmically
from
rim to rim.
Trailing a message
a memory, a meaning
of
being
heard
of being rendered
of being curious
to follow the pencil's lead
of leaded footsteps'
curls and lines abstracting
visualization
visualizing abstractions
oh hail, the wand of writing.

Heidi Simmons

Ode to Bacon

Greasy, fatty
perfection
perfect with pancakes
superb with syrup
I worship you
amazing bacon.
Turkey or pig
it does
not
matter
as long as
its
BACON!

Josh, 5th grade

Ode to a Chair

My chair waits for me
everyday
with its armrests
comfortable backrest.
The one who is my
thinking chair
throne of power to control myself
seat for meditation
relaxation
become a king of my life
when sitting on
that chair
A warm feeling
transports me to another land
of my command
where I can live freely
in my fantasy world
but then
reality wakes me up
as I realize
I am still
grounded.

Adam 5th grade

Ode to a Snake

Snake
smooth
scaly line
twisting
sliding
unseen.
Narrowed eyes
burning holes through the air.
Slipping silently
through the crunchy leaves.
Forked tongue flicking
in and out
a mouse scuttles past.
Head snapping forward
Striking.
Slinking forward
in a long scaly line.

Katya, 4th grade

Ode to Backpacks

Torn out, frayed, but still faithful
clinging to my back
worn high with pride
my companion
patterns faded
my only friend
that is willing to be
my pack mule.
ode to you
staying strong
I am sorry
for not giving you
the proper amount of respect.
Shame on me for overloading you
I am your companion
after all.

Sabrina, 5th grade

Ode to a Pig

Pig
your pink, oink noise
when you run
through the grass fields
your pink pale skin
with your curly noodle tail
your circle nose with little holes.
your crisp bacon
that I adore.

Zoe, 4th grade

Ode to Snow

Oh snow
you turn the image of the
naked trees
and
gloomy grass
into
an enchanted forest
of white heaven
with
different snow flakes
to make
something the same.

Sam, 5th grade

Ode to Being Alone

If you are alone
you know how I feel
being alone
is peace
quiet
you enjoy it
never annoying
never sad
always happy
as you fall into
your nightly slumber.

Alexandria, 5th grade

Ode to an Empty Mind

Blank,
Blank as glistening
snow.
A blank sheet of paper.
An infinite
universe
free of thought!
Ideas trapped
by the
ever - growing
darkness of
nothing
But even
in nothing
something
happens!

Elijah, 4th grade

Ode to a Star

"Sparkle Sparkle"

of the star
so bright
in the soulless dark night
twirling and dancing
every day in different
worlds
side to side
all universe long
never stop
no thinking just
flowing
in the soulless dark night.

Victoria, 4th grade

Ode to a Fox

Slinking forward
light paws pattering the ground
bushy tail, flicking back and forth
long fiery red fur
ruffled in the wind
curved silver claws
sinking into crumbly
dirt
pierced perky ears twitching
small paws silently running through
light green grass
dark calm eyes staring forward
unmoving.
                    Katya, 4th grade

Ode to a Gecko

Short spotted gecko
slowly climbing upward
sticky toes
grasping a tree
head slowly moving
side to side
slippery skin
sharp eyes flickering about
                    Katya, 5th grade

Glorious Chocolate

Chocolate, O Glorious Chocolate,
Sweet and delicious,
Yummy and dark,
You bring me joy and happiness.
You are so delicious and glorious.
Don't leave me, for you are my savior food.

Glorious Chocolate, when you crunch between my teeth, you are hard,
But when you get fully in my mouth, you start to dissolve.
As you slowly flatten on my tongue, and I suck you down
I immediately want more.

Chocolate, O Glorious Chocolate,
When I eat you, I feel up and ready to go.
Glorious Chocolate, you make me feel happy, proud, lovely, gorgeous, and loud.
Chocolate, O Glorious Chocolate, you are my savior food.
                    Delanie, 3rd grade

BIBLIOGRAPHY

1) Neruda, Pablo. (1994). *Ode To Common Things*. NY, NY: Bulfinch.
2) Neruda, Pablo. (1994). *Ode To Opposites*. NY, NY: Bulfinch.
3) Soto, Gary. (1992). *Neighborhood Odes*. NY, NY: Harcourt.
4) Janeczko, Paul. (2005) *A Kick In the Head*. Cambridge, MA: Candlewick Press.

Session 2: HAIKU

Materials needed:
- *Examples and observations from* The Haiku Picture Book For Children *(in bibliography)*
- *Mentor text examples stated below*
- **Haiku** *activity sheet (self-explanatory)*

DESCRIPTION

- Haiku is a Japanese art form where language and content are of greatest importance. In haiku, a poet's focus is on a moment in nature that has been observed or participated in. A haiku is made up of three lines and incomplete sentences. Few adjectives are used and no metaphors or similes. A haiku is a literal reverence of a noticed moment. Most important is that the poet allows time to **notice,** observe, and celebrate a moment that is most likely missed when rushing through life.

- A traditional haiku consists of five syllables in the first line; seven syllables in the second; and again five in the last line. This is a rule to be broken more than adhered to, as it can inhibit the spontaneity of the moment, especially for the beginner. Having only three lines is a rule that can make the exercise less daunting. Below are examples of haiku that have been translated from Japanese and are not 5-7-5.

- As well, there are examples from children who read the mentor text examples and were able to generalize the purpose, implement the idea, and experience the reward of writing haiku.

EXAMPLES

Buson, one of the most famous haikuists, wrote the following haiku after noticing a red turnip in the winter river:

> In the winter river
> Pulled up and thrown away
> a red turnip.
>   Buson

Then he noticed the cherry trees standing in blossom at the end of spring:

> Departing Spring
> Hesitates
> In the late cherry blossoms.
>   Buson

On noticing a spider web in the early morning dew:

> Morning spider
> hangs a web
> strings of dew
>
>> Heidi Simmons

On noticing a wave lapping at the shoreline:

> Waves ebb
> leaving froth
> on smooth sand
>
>> Heidi Simmons

On noticing a squirrel in the fall:

> A squirrel
> gently paws
> a rolling nut.
>
>> Allison, 5th grade

On noticing a cicada singing:

> The cicada
> hides itself
> then comes out to sing.
>
>> Adam, 5th grade

On noticing seaweed at the beach:

> Green seaweed
> nature's sway
> tiny Tornadoes
>
>> Lili, 5th, grade

On seeing redwoods in California:

> Redwood
> towering above me
> motionless
>
>> Sadie, 5th grade

On watching a tiny ant:

> Tiny Ant
> guards the doors
> to Queen Ant's castle
>
>> Lili, 5th grade

BIBLIOGRAPHY

1) Nishimoto, Keisuke. (1998). *Haiku Picture Book for Children*. Compton, CA: Heian International.
2) Janeczko, Paul. (2005). *A Kick In the Head*. Cambridge, MA: Candlewick Press.
3) Neruda, Pablo. (1994). *Ode to Common Things*. NY, NY: Bullfinch.

Session 3: CINQUAIN

DESCRIPTION

- A cinquain has five lines with a format of 2, 4, 6, 8, 2, of respective syllables in each line. The poem is a message about something that poets know well. In fact, better than other people because of special experiences that they have had. It is like a haiku in that it captures a personal moment.
- The cinquain does not have obvious rhymes. If a rhyme occurs, it was not intended. It naturally evolved, because it was the right word.

EXAMPLES

Sisters

Joined by
a birthing in
a family, but then
apart by anger nesting in
mind's eye.

Heidi Simmons

A Bike

Pedals
two handle bars
pedals, chain reaction
the bike is a giant puzzle
it taunts

Eijiah, 4th grade

Chocolate Crumbs

Little
small crumbs bouncing
falling from the sky high
child's chocolate cookies very
yummy

Allison, 5th grade

Rowing

As glass
the water is
a sheet of flat stillness.
Rhythmic punches plunge holes of sweat
and strain.

Heidi Simmons

BIBLIOGRAPHY:

1. Janeczko, Paul. (2005) *A Kick In the Head*. Cambridge, MA: Candlewick Press.

Session 4: ALLITERATION, ASSONANCE, and CONSONANCE

Materials required:
- **Alliteration** *activity sheet (Self-explanatory)*

GENERAL DESCRIPTION

- These are not particular forms of poetry, like Ode, Haiku, or Cinquain, but **strategies** that can be used to make poetry and any writing more pleasing.

ALLITERATION DESCRIPTION

- **Alliteration** is the repetition of initial consonant sounds of words.
- The repeated sound does not have to occur in the same line. It can appear throughout a poem, which is more subtle and can be particularly effective.
- When reading a child's poem, acknowledge it or look for opportunities to encourage alliteration.

ALLITERATION EXAMPLES

Purple Dispersion

A plum of purple
splattered on the walls
fairies scattered in every direction
a purple bed plopped in the corner of the room
with fuzzy covers
everything
purple in my room.

Sophia, 5th grade

Whistle and Whirl

Whistle and whirl of the wind
the leaves dance with flowers
and
they jump and tear together
suddenly
the rain comes fluttering down
flash goes the thunder
tears with the leaves
the wind whistles
and whirls
again
and
again
then everything goes
STILL
"app-a-loot-ley" (absolutely)
STILL.

Phoebe, 2nd grade

Dawn

At the break of dawn
Dew shimmers and shakes on
the emerald green grass.

Birds call out warning
calls as a fiery colored fox
slinks out of a bristly bush
silent on its quick light paws.

Squirrels scuttle cautiously
Through the underbrush scavenging
for food.

A small dappled fawn
steps slowly over a log and
bounds off.

Dew shimmers and shakes
On the emerald green grass
at the break of dawn.

Katya, 4th grade

ASSONANCE DESCRIPTION

Repetitive sounds do not only have to occur at the beginning of a word to make the poem or piece of writing pleasing to hear and pleasant to comprehend.

There is the strategy of **assonance** where repetitive vowel sounds found within the words rhyme and have the same pleasing effect as alliteration. When you see assonance in a student's work, acknowledge and encourage it.

ASSONANCE EXAMPLE *(marked in bold)*

The Storm

The bl**u**nder sl**u**nder of the st**o**rm
as it blows hard through the trees
wildly
the day is dark black
all day long.

The sl**u**nder d**u**nder of the st**o**rm
the th**u**nder as it r**o**lls past my **eyes**
the bl**u**nder sl**u**nder of the storm
as the rain cr**ies.**

The trees have fl**it** bl**it**
sha**king** and thro**wing** leaves
as **it is**
a black day on Monday.

Melissa, 2nd grade

CONSONANCE DESCRIPTION

- Also, there is the strategy of **consonance** where the consonant sound does not repeat itself in the beginning of the word as in alliteration, but in the middle or at the end of the word. Young students have an affinity for this kind of sound repetition. It is found in nursery rhymes and songs on the playground, which are easily remembered and recited.
- Teachers need to acknowledge this in their students' writing. One best instructs sound strategies through awareness and relishing the pleasure of its rhythm and sound.

CONSONANCE EXAMPLE *The sound of /s/ throughout the poem gives the reader a pleasant rhythm and focus.*

Escaping Fish

With a **s**plash
the orange fish
jump**s** out
twi**s**ting in the air
slapping down
on a **s**mooth
surface
struggling
floundering
ga**s**ping
THEN
gently
lifted back
to the **s**afety
of
the cold aquarium water

Katya, 4th grade

[There is no specific extended bibliography for this session.]

Session 5: ONOMATOPOEIA

DESCRIPTION

- Onomatopoeia is another strategy that can be used to make poetry and any writing both rhythmic and fun sounding. It is the formation of a word, as *cuckoo, meow, honk*, or *boom*, which is the imitation of a sound made by or associated with its referent. In other words, it sounds like its meaning.
- It is difficult to describe but very easy for young students to create.
- Children naturally use onomatopoeia to reference the world. It is sufficient to note that this is an effective writing strategy and encourage students to create other examples of onomatopoeia strategies.

EXAMPLES

Leaves

Leaves floating
fluttering
in the air
sway and dance
of the leaves
quiet of the leaves
crunch
crunch
of stepping on the leaves
rustle of the leaves
swish, swash of the leaves
rustle of the leaves.

Monet, 2nd grade

Shooting A Basket

The shooting, **whooshing, swooshing** ball
arching into the basket
rolls round and round the rim
teasing teammates
then
d
r
o
p
s
neatly through the net.
YES!

Yaxel, 3rd grade

Rain

**P-lip p-lop plippty p-lop
blup**
a
rain
drop
bounces off
an umbrella
plop on the cement it goes.

Lia, 2nd grade

Little Mouse

Tsk, tsk, tsk
of a tiny
mouse
was greeting
his mouslings
in the alley
**hissity, hiss, hiss
hisses** the alley cat
trying to catch
his prey.

Mary, 3rd grade

[There is no specific extended bibliography for this session.]

Name _____

Haiku Activity Sheet

Observe a moment that you think is quite wonderful and perhaps no one else has noticed. Write it in three short lines.

I noticed: _____

_____

_____

The haiku I wrote was: _____

_____

_____

I noticed: _____

_____

_____

The haiku I wrote was: _____

_____

_____

I noticed: _____

_____

_____

The haiku I wrote was: _____

_____

_____

Name _____

Alliteration Activity Sheet

This is a fun sheet for practicing Alliteration. Alliteration is the repetition of beginning consonant sounds. ***Alliteration does not use repetitive vowels.***

B is because, before, between, but....but

_____

C can cuddle and caress and seem so caring then canter quickly away

_____

D dives into danger or dries up in a drought

_____

F feigns feelings unless tickled with a feather

_____

G grinds and grabs then gives back gently

_____

H hushes hollow halos honorably

_____

J just just

_____

K kills with careful kindness

_____

L clucks, lolls, laps delicious

_____

M meshed lips, hmmmmmmms melodies

_____

N nips, nabs, needles unnecessarily

_____

Continue playing with the rest of the consonants using alliteration. Go back and use the consonants that have already been played with. Thumb through a dictionary to get ideas for words.

P_____

Q_____

R_____

S_____

T_____

V_____

W_____

X_____

Z_____

Alliteration Word Splash

Choose a consonant that you "love" to make with your lips and tongue. Then find three to five nouns, verbs and describing words that begin with that sound. From this word splash make a poem. One does not have to use all the words.

NOUNS	VERBS	Describing Words

Example:

I chose "S." I found lots of "s" words I liked by flipping through the "s" part of the dictionary, used a thesaurus and finally decided to use these words:

safe	sail	saint
sensitive	simmer	stain
serene	sashay	sunburn
sinister	scare	surprise
scratch	seduce	sun

My final poem using these words is below:

The Sinister Sun

How **sinister** is the **sun**
to appear **so serene**
sashaying sweetly across the **sky**
seducing us to bask
in its ravishing ray**s**
and all the while **staining sensitive skin**
with **sunscald.**

✦ Creating a Poetry Resource

WHY THIS RESOURCE

During the last eight lessons, students have built a curiosity for words, explored their significance and established an independent competence. In turn, teachers have realized the potential of students' **word awareness development** and its impact on their intellectual growth. To continue this enthusiastic and rewarding engagement with language, teachers need to find a place for poetry in their ongoing literacy curriculum.

This addendum instructs the creation of a resource that will build and challenge students' evolving word awareness as well as further an understanding of their inner self and a communication with their outer world.

The instruction of five poems is modeled below. Teachers can use these models and then create an invaluable resource by collecting and preparing a study of poems of their choice.

In this instruction students:

- Practice individual and choral read-aloud.
- Acknowledge rhythm and word choice.
- Discover new language.
- Find heart in the message.
- Analyze word meaning.
- Recognize poetic elements.
- Are inspired to create original writing.

Suggestions for instruction are two-tiered.
Introduce each poem using these steps

- Go over all the vocabulary that is difficult to pronounce or understand.
- Read the poem to the class.
- Have the class read the poem all together.
- Have students volunteer to maestro the poem.
- Encourage students to underline words or phrases that they particularly like.

Create applicable activities using the following considerations:

- Consider the "why" of the title.
- Notice the familiar poetic elements of rhythm; image and comparison; word choice; heart and message.
- Notice poetic and rich language.

- Consider students' connection to the poem.
- Write an original poem, inspired from the message, the words, or the structure.

POEM 1

Mother To Son

Langston Hughes

Well, son, I'll tell you:
Life for me ain't been no crystal stair,
It's had tacks in it,
And splinters,
And boards torn up,
And places with no carpet on the floor-
Bare.
But all the time
I'se been a-climbin' on,
And reachin' landin's,
And turnin' corners,
And sometimes goin' in the dark
Where there ain't been no light.
So boy, don't you turn back.
Don't you set down on the steps
'Cause you finds it's kinder hard.
Don't you fall now-
For I'se still goin', honey,
I'se still climbin',
And life for me ain't been no crystal stair.

Discussion/Activity Ideas

The Title
- Who is talking to whom? How old do you think the son might be?

Poetic Elements
- Comparisons and message can be presented through the vocabulary discussion below.

Vocabulary/Poetic language
- What is crystal? Pair share: If you walked into a house and saw a flight of crystal stairs, where do you think they would lead you?

- In line *2*, what is *"life"* compared to? Describe a crystal stair and explain what a life like a crystal stair might be like. Would you like a crystal stair life? Has the mother had a life like a crystal stair?
- In lines 4, 5, 6, 7, she tells the kind of stairs in her life. What are they? What do her bare stairs with splinters, boards, and no carpets tell us about her life? Is she saying that when she walks along she runs into splinters and tacks?
- In lines 8, 9, we find out how she deals with these lousy stairs. How does she?
- When we read lines 10, 11, 12, 13, how do we know that sometimes life has been hard for her? What does she mean when she says she has been places where there just isn't any light?
- In lines 14, 15, 16, 17, what is her message to her son?
- In lines 18, 19, 20, she tells us what she will continue to do. What is it?
- Do you think she will ever have an opportunity to climb a crystal stair?

Connection
- Do you think your life is a crystal stair?
- What kind of stair would you compare your life to?

Make a suggestion for writing a poem similar to this poem
- Have the children write one paragraph about a time their life that has been like a crystal stair.
- And one paragraph about a time in life that has been like a ragged rug stair.
- Have the students make a comparative list of what a crystal stair of life might look like compared to a stair that is a ragged rug stair of life.
- Showing them the model below or something self-written, have the children underline ideas in their paragraphs that they might include in a poem.

EXAMPLE

The Ragged and Crystal Stair

Life is a crystal stair with
a velvet carpet
as my daughter finds a man
who gives her a ring
that decorates her hand
forever
he promises.

Life is a crystal stair with
sparkles and shine
when my son has a job
that gives him smiles
and dollars.

Life is a crystal stair with
a smooth rail and easy steps
when I come to a class and
children beam with tomorrow's learning.

and
then
there is a tack
a rumpled rug
I trip
and scrape my knee.
My dog Bailey Boy hurts
he breathes hard
I cannot fix him.

There is no railing
I wobble side to side
with no support.
My sisters said they loved me only
as a child and
have left.
I fall and grab out
for my mother
but she has passed.

I lay crumpled on the stairs
once crystal

but even though it's kinda hard
I will be climbin' on
I will not fall
I CAN climb the stair
and find
my way.

Heidi Simmons

POEM 2

The Bully

Bobby Nelson is the toughest kid in our class
I am the smallest.
His hoarse voice finds me every day
on the way to school and home again..
"Hey Rabbit, whatcha doin'?"
A rock drops into my gut.
He walks next to me,
throws his elbow into my ribs and edges me to the curb
hoping I will take a swing at him.
I tried once and he flipped
me like a toy dog.

One day Jim, my best friend, gets fed up
with Nelson's jabs and taunts.
Someone on the playground yells "fight"
and a ring of kids surrounds them.
"Hit 'im, Jim."
"Take him, Nelson."
saying, "Yeah,Yeah, Yeah,
think you're big,
think you're tough."
Nelson takes a swing;
Jim catches his arm
and twists him to the ground;
the dust flies, the circle cheers
Jim sits on Nelson
like we own the playground
the school and everything in it.

Donald Graves

Discussion/Activity Ideas

The Title
- Who is the bully? Why is he a bully?

Poetic Elements rhythm; image and comparison; word choice; heart and message
- Where can you find the "heart" expressed in this poem.
- What is the strongest image in this poem?
- What do you think Ralph Fletcher's message is in this poem?

Vocabulary/Poetic language
Look at the words Fletcher used in this poem and compare them to synonyms he could have used. Discuss why you think he chose the words he did.
- in line 2, "hoarse voice" instead of "mean voice"
- in line 8, "throws his elbow" instead of "pokes his elbow"
- in line 11, "flipped" instead of "throw me down"
- in line 12, "gets fed up" instead of "gets mad"
- in line 18, "shoves back and forth" instead of "begins to fight"
- in line 25, "the dust flies and the circle cheers"

Connection
- Have you ever experienced bullying yourself or watched it happen?

Make a suggestion for writing a poem similar to this poem
- Donald Graves has written a poem. The poem almost sounds like a story but it has rhythm and poetic language.
- Have the students think of a focused moment that has happened to them and a friend at school. Write a story poem like Fletcher has.
- Brainstorm some possible focused moments: e.g. sharing a snack; being left out of a game; sharing a secret; being bullied: loving the same hobby.

POEM 3

SHOES

[**NOTE**: Please look in the Valerie Worth *Small Poems* book for a copy of the poem, *Shoes*.]

Discussion/Activity Ideas

The Title

- Do you think this is the best title for this poem? Why or why not?

Poetic Elements: rhythm; image and comparison; word choice; heart and message

- Rhythm is achieved through some poetic strategies. Help the students find examples of **Alliteration:** *hard heels; smooth, soft, supple, summer; carved, clacked.*
- And **Consonance:** *thick, like, rock, waxed, clack*
- Worth has used words that make the shoes seem to come alive. Her words seem to personify the shoes. What words are those?
- Worth's vocabulary is rich and visual. Ask the students to draw the images she creates of the different shoes.

Vocabulary/Poetic language

- What words help us to feel the hardness of the shoe: *hard, leather, blocks, carved, thick, waxed, wood.* All use hard consonants.
- Why do you think the author used "pale soles" of sneakers and not just "white sole"? Pale and sole have consonance, pale is a more specific color and makes the sneaker seem like human skin.

Connection

- With which shoe do you most closely connect?

Make a suggestion for writing a poem similar to this poem

- Choose two pairs of shoes from your house. Make sure that they are different enough to compare and contrast with each other.

POEM 4

DREAMS

Dreams
To fling my arms wide
In some place in the sun
To whirl and to dance
Till the white day is done.
Then rest at cool evening
Beneath a tall tree
While night comes on gently
Dark like me-
That is my dream!

To fling my arms wide
In the face of the sun
Dance! Whirl! Whirl!
Till the quick day is done
Rest at pale evening......
A tall slim tree.....
Night come tenderly
      Black like me.

Langston Hughes

Discussion/Activity Ideas

The Title
- Why is **Dreams** a good title for this poem?
- Can a dream become real?

Poetic Elements: rhythm; image and comparison; word choice; heart and message

- What are the ways that this poem has rhythm? **Alliteration:** *wide, whirl, white, while.* **Rhyme:** *tree, gently, me; tree, tenderly, me.* **Repetition:** *To fling my arms wide.*
- What do the images of white and darkness communicate?
- What words does he use to show that this poem is full of heart?
- What adjectives does he use to personify day and how are they different from the ones that he uses to personify night?
- Hughes is proud to be a Black man. Where is this message clear in his poem?

Vocabulary/Poetic language

- What does a "white day" look like?
- Is a cool evening the same as a pale evening?
- Why might he use "fling" his arms and not "open" his arms?
- Is night or day quicker according to the last stanza?
- The poet says that the night comes on tenderly and gently. Find this in the poem.
- What would a night look like that came on harshly and brutally?
- How do we know the poet thinks he is like the night?
- How is the first stanza like the second stanza?

Connection

- What are your dreams? Make a list of ten of them.

Suggestions for writing a poem similar to this poem

- Choose the very most important dream from your list.
- Begin a poem: *To fling my arms wide*
- Use *to fling my arms wide* twice in your poem just like Langston Hughes.

POEM 5

MY DOG, HE IS AN UGLY DOG

[**NOTE**: This Jack Prelutsky poem is available both on the Internet and listed in the **(R)** Required books in the bibliography.]

Discussion/Activity Ideas

The Title

- Does the title tell the reader the true feelings of the poet?

Poetic Elements: rhythm; image and comparison; word choice; heart and message

- What are the ways that this poem has rhythm: **rhyme; repetition; alliteration?**
- The image of the "ugly dog" is clear. Draw a picture of the dog that Jack Prelutsky describes.
- What are the comparisons used to communicate the image?
- The poet constantly criticizes his dog, but you know that he loves the dog. How do you know that this is a poem filled with heart?

Vocabulary/Poetic language

- How do you know what the word *scruffy* means by not looking it up in the dictionary?
- Why are "slow" and "thick" descriptive words for "stupid"?

Connection

- Do you have something that everyone else thinks is ugly but is beautiful to you, e.g. a pet, a hat, a shirt, a bike, a haircut?
- Share the ideas with the whole class and to inspire fellow classmates.

Suggestion for writing a poem similar to this poem

- From the list of your connections, write a poem similar to *My Dog, He Is an Ugly Dog*.
- Explain all the reasons you think that your choice may be ugly, like Pretlutsky did, and at the end exclaim that is exactly why you love it so much!

✦ Self-Initiated Examples from Students Well-Practiced in Their Poetry Efforts

WHY THESE EXAMPLES

Once children are well practiced and successful in their writing of poetry, they can find inspiration, appropriate structure and a focus independent of explicit teaching. At this point poetry becomes an important tool for students' self-discovery and worldly communication.

The following are some examples of unsolicited poetry written by students who experienced the instruction from the lessons of this book.

EXAMPLE 1: Emotional Reactions to a Social Studies Unit.

Jim Crow

Jim Crow
you have been as bad as you know
mocking the Blacks
acting rude
and giving all Blacks
attitude.
Maybe if you will stop now
your seed of goodness will show.

Jim Crow, Jim Crow
you need to stop.
This is no fun and games.
Do I have to call the cops?
You hurt the Blacks emotionally.

acting rude
and giving all Blacks
attitude.
Maybe if you will stop now
your seed of goodness will show.

Jim Crow, Jim Crow
you need to stop.
This is no fun and games.

Do I have to call the cops?
You hurt the Blacks emotionally.
Something you cannot see.

Jim Crow, Jim Crow
this is not fun.
You are ruining everything
for everyone.
You think you're cool but
you are just a fool
mocking differences

Jim Crow, Jim Crow
there should be a law
I just wish other people saw
I am not kidding
I am not joking
you need to stop
RIGHT NOW!

Avery, 4th grade

The Amistad

Strugglers
Over the seas
Suddenly
Clash! Fighting
For dear life
New orders
To turn around
To Africa
By day.
North by
The crack of night.
Spaniard
Voyage to New London
Arrived
Custom House
To court we
Will all go
Again and again
Loss to loss
To jail
For both of us.

Joseph, 5th grade

Their Voice

No!
They cried
In their native language
As they were taken away from their homes

But they were carried by ship to Cuba

Steer us home
They commanded
Through gestures and unknown words
As they revolted and overthrew

But the crew zigzagged up the American coast

Let us free
They pleaded
With their newfound English
As their case was tried in court

And in the end they were set free

Ellanora, 5th grade

EXAMPLE 2: Heartfelt Memories

My Baby

Slumped in the blue cloth chair
in a dark corner.
Forgotten
I rarely dress her
but I always keep her in my sight
close to me
Free from dust
these years.
Now and then I pick her up
stroke her smooth
multicolored head from
the many-marker tattoos
I penned permanently on her face
and arms.

Meg, 5th grade

My Blanket

My blanket
so soft from years of use
knotted stitches of yarn
fuzzy pink, white, blue, yellow and
green folds
warm my insides
every night.

Meg, 5th grade

EXAMPLE 3: Sharing and Purging Sadness

A Waterfall of Tears

A waterfall of tears
All that is left is her empty cage
with her favorite belongings
Everywhere I look I see her
I think about her all the time
Wishing she was here
She will be buried in the garden
with her bed and chew toy
so in spring flowers will grow
beside herself.

Adam, 5th grade

The Letter

My dad wrote me a sad letter
It was sad because
He wrote he was 'gonna' come out
in a couple of years

The last letter he wrote us
said he would be out
in a couple of months

Sometimes I don't like cops

I got so mad
when I read that

"NO"
I yelled
"I can't take this anymore."

Nelvin, 4th grade

Flaws

Just because of my appearance
doesn't mean I'm not
a regular kid
without a friend
waiting for a friend.
I don't want to be ridiculed
or teased
or ignored
I shouldn't be judged
by my outside
but by my inside.
If I was seen by my inside
I would have friends
or a friend
to play with.

Lucas, 4th grade

EXAMPLE 4: Moments Recreated with Sensational Precision

Nail Salon

The nail salon
snip, snip, snipping of nail clippers
tick, tick ticking of clocks
behold the tall black shelf
filled with hundreds
of different colors of nail polish
I want a silvery grey,
light pink or sparkly purple
still scanning
losing patience

I'm called
Jump up
I feel the warm leather chair
vibrating under me
relaxed and comfortable
the clear coat is stroked on
the hot air dryer
hardens my nails
I get a glimpse of the sparkly purple
and I think
it was worth waiting for

Sequoia, 5th grade

Rubber band

Literacy fades away
as the bending
twisting maze of rubber band
entwines my fingers
as it pulls me
from the real world.

I plummet deeper into my thoughts
of candy cane forests and peppermint stepping stones
of cotton candy and Hersey's kisses hail.

Kora
my name echoes in meaningless reality,
Kora
I somehow float to the surface
of the real world from the depths of
my thoughts.

My eyes snap open
I look around the empty classroom.
Mary is standing in the doorway
saying
"Kora, everyone has gone to lunch!"

Kora, 4th grade

The Beach

At the beach
in the summer
the water is shiny and warm
the waves go sky high
then splash and splatter

Annaelise, 3rd grade

EXAMPLE 5: Celebrating Relationships with Pets

Dulche

My big furry ball
hops up
sleeps at the foot of my bed
sometimes
squirms up to my armpit
nestles, firmly in
her snores
lull me to sleep
happiness.

Eddie, 5th grade

My Luna

My Luna follows me everywhere
licking me, bumping
asking for attention
so beautiful and chocolatey brown
And
when we play together
time stops
the world stops spinning
it's just us together
we run, we wrestle
And
at night we are together
as she lays on my carpet
my little Luna
And
I wake up
she races to me
and licks me until I laugh
And
then I hug, and rub her
that lovely, silky, amazing dog
named Luna
and it pains me to leave her.
Every day
when I get home
she nudges me to the yard
to play again
my Luna.

Josh, 5th grade

EXAMPLE 6: Messaging with Teachers

Free Write Jail

The second
Ms. Heidi
tells me to write a haiku
I'm a prisoner of writing.

Wanting to get out
blocked by Ms. Heidi
frustrated that I have to obey.
No memory of anything
except for words.
I'm a prisoner of writing.

Almost free
once
free-write is over
but until then
I'm a prisoner of writing.

I wonder
what other people she keeps
in the writing jail cells.

I fantasize
that Ms. Heidi is the warden
putting kids like me
in jail cells
because they are unbearable
saying they can't write
saying they're bad
at writing.
She chuckles
and says,
"Go write a story, a poem, anything."

And I try
but
I never succeed.

                              Hannah, 5th grade

Poetry.....Not fun

Poetry is
Not fun.
Not a cool boy
Not a great friend
Just not fun
Poetry is
A bore
A yawn catcher
A sleep magnet
Just not fun.
You read verses
I don't listen
I write words
You claim is poetry
It's just not fun
Really
Poetry is
Not fun.

Joey, 4th grade

The Positive of Everything

Ms. Heidi, Ms. Heidi
you are the sun
that brightens the world
and helps achieve
greatness.
You are the words
to a poem
the faithful honest
meaning of creativity.
You are a role model
to students
young and old
certainly an inspiration
to me.
Ms. Heidi, Ms. Heidi
you will always
be in my
heart.

Maliyah, 5th grade

Bibliography

*Some texts are required and necessary for instructing these lessons. Those with an **(R)** beside them, are **required**. Those texts with an **(S)**, **suggested,** are mentioned or used in the lesson and would be very good to add to a class library, but are not necessary for teaching the lesson.*

A complete Bibliography is arranged alphabetically by Lesson, followed by a List of Required Mentor Texts.

Lesson 1
(S) Fletcher, Ralph. (2005). *A Writing Kind of Day,* Honesdale, PA: Boyds Mill.
(S) Graves, Donald. (1996). *Baseball, Snakes and Summer Squash,* Honesdale, PA: Boyds Mills.
(S) Hughes, Langston. (1994). *Dream Keeper,* NY, NY: Alfred Knopf.
(S) Prelutsky, Jack. (1991). *The New Kid On The Block,* NY, NY: Alfred A. Knopf.

Lesson 3
(R) Yolen, Jane. (1987). *Owl Moon.* NY, NY: Philomel.
(R) Zolotow, Charlotte. (1992). *The Seashore Book,* NY, NY: Harper Collins.

Lesson 4
(S) Hughes, Langston. (1994). *Dream Keeper,* NY, NY: Alfred Knopf.
(R) Magnetic poetry kit (order from Amazon.com)
(S) Rowling, J.K. (1997). *Harry Potter* NY, NY: Scholastic.
(S) White, E.B. (1952). *Charlotte's Web,* NY, NY: Harper Collins.
(S) Worth, Valerie. (1987). *All The Small Poems,* NY, NY: Harper Collins.

Lesson 5
(S) Gendler, Ruth (1988). *The Book of Qualities,* NY, NY: Harper Collins.
(R) Kipfer, Barbara, A. (2011). *Roget's International Thesaurus, 7th Edition,* NY, NY: Harper Collins.
(S) White, E.B. (1952). *Charlotte's Web,* NY, NY: Harper Collins.

Lesson 6
(R) Carlstrom, Nancy. (1993). *How Does The Wind Walk,* NY, NY: MacMillan.
(R) Fletcher, Ralph. (1997). *Twilight Comes Twice,* NY, NY: Houghton Mifflin Harcourt.
(R) Sidman, Joyce. (2009). *Red Sings From Treetops,* NY, NY: Houghton Mifflin Harcourt.
(S) Worth, Valerie. (1987). *All The Small Poems,* NY, NY: Harper Collins.

Lesson 8

(S) Janeczko, Paul. (2005). *A Kick In the Head*, Cambridge MA: Candlewick Press.

(R) Neruda, Pablo (1994). *Ode to Common Things*, NY, NY: Bullfinch.

(R) Nishimoto, Keisuke, (1998). *Haiku Picture Book for Children*, Compton, CA: Heian International.

Creating A Poetry Resource

(S) Graves, Donald. (1996). *Baseball, Snakes and Summer Squash*, Honesdale, PA: Boyds Mills.

(S) Hughes, Langston. (1994). *Dream Keeper*, NY, NY: Alfred Knopf.

(R) Worth, Valerie. (1987). *All The Small Poems*, NY, NY: Harper Collins.

(R) Prelutsky, Jack. (1991). *The New Kid On The Block*, NY, NY: Alfred A. Knopf.

List of Required Mentor Texts and Resources

Lesson 3:   Yolen, Jane. (1987). *Owl Moon*. NY, NY: Philomel.

Zolotow, Charlotte. (1992). *The Seashore Book*, NY, NY: Harper Collins.

Lesson 4:   Magnetic Poetry kit (Order from Amazon.com).

Lesson 5:   Kipfer, Barbara A. (2011). *Roget's International Thesaurus, 7th Edition*, NY, NY: Harper Collins.

Lesson 6:   Carlstrom, Nancy. (1993). *How Does The Wind Walk*, NY, NY: MacMillan.

Lesson 6:   Fletcher, Ralph. (1997). *Twilight Comes Twice*, NY, NY: Houghton Mifflin Harcourt.

Lesson 6:   Sidman, Joyce. (2009). *Red Sings From Treetops*, NY, NY: Houghton Mifflin Harcourt.

Lesson 8:   Neruda, Pablo (1994). *Ode to Common Things*, NY, NY: Bullfinch.

Lesson 8:   Nishimoto, Keisuke, (1998). *Haiku Picture Book for Children*, Compton, CA: Heian International.

**Creating
A Poetry
Resource :**   Prelutsky, Jack. (1991). *The New Kid On The Block*, NY, NY: Alfred A.Knopf.

Worth, Valerie. (1987). *All The Small Poems*, NY, NY: Harper Collins.

Acknowledgments

They say it "takes a village to raise a child." As well it has taken a village to create this book. Hopefully it will help writing teachers raise a new generation of young students to use poetry to discover word meaning and love writing.

Thanks go to The Regional Multicultural Magnet School in New London, Connecticut, for encouraging me to explore the use of poetry for a child's writing success. Those teachers who welcomed me into their classrooms over the years were Lynn Hancock, Stacy Pleau-Guckian, Kristin Gemaly, Chrismae Gooden-White, Liz Quinones, Joanne Huber-Williston, Lucy Regan, Debbie Guinan-Morizio, Kelley Norcia, Ellen Hill and Donna Showers. Their classes were intellectual incubators where these lessons were first introduced. The successes we achieved are collected in this book.

My long-time buddy Dorothy Papp entered into this "village" as an educator, a lover of language and an asker of "why!" She painstakingly combed through the book's text and language message and then asked "why." When I didn't have an answer the lesson was changed.

A fellow traveler, Kate Mercer, understood and visually interpreted my message throughout the book and on the cover.

My dearest friend Nancy Wright, a fellow teacher of diverse student populations, continually encouraged me to finish the book and assured me it was a needed resource.

Another more recent friend, Elsa Colligan, began writing poetry at age ten and published in her thirties. Today in her nineties, she actively writes and publishes. Elsa is an inspiration who celebrates her poetic life every day. It expands her vocabulary, empowers her life, and her poetry becomes bolder, wilder and deeper.

Publisher Grace Peirce patiently guided me through the complex publishing process and showed me how to use social media to spread learning.

My children Jane Simmons Meiser and Robert Waldo Simmons who from their first baby "babble" to their later creations of metaphor, revealed the natal quality of poetry and its positive impact on their writing competency.

While my name is on the cover of the book, and I take full responsibility for its shortcomings, I thank all of the "villagers" once again for their love and support.

About the Author

Heidi Simmons was the K-5 Literacy Coach at the Regional Multicultural Magnet School in New London, Connecticut, for many years. While there, her students won numerous prizes from the Connecticut Writing Project. She also taught writing to adolescents, undergraduates, and graduate students at home and in Taiwan, China, where she lived for three years. She received her BS in Early Childhood Education from Wheelock College, a Masters in History from Northeastern and another Masters in Literacy from the University of Rhode Island. More recently she was a pre-doctoral candidate in Education at Lesley University. Through a combination of academic research and extensive teaching experience, she has created a book that helps teachers replicate her poetic approach to a child's word meaning development and written expression.